TREASURE
– *in* –
EARTHEN
VESSELS

Prayer & the Embodied Life

TREASURE
– in –
EARTHEN VESSELS

Prayer & the Embodied Life

Dn. Stephen Muse

SAINT TIKHON'S

MONASTERY
P·R·E·S·S

MMXVII

Treasure in Earthen Vessels

Published by:
St. Tikhon's Monastery Press
175 St. Tikhon's Road
Waymart, Pennsylvania 18472
Printed in the United States of America

ISBN: 978-0-9974718-5-4

PRAISE FOR *Treasure in Earthen Vessels*

When reading this book, I felt as though I was eavesdropping on a prayer, reflective of the author's life-long witness to God's healing work with men and women of faith. Dn. Stephen offers a rare, intimate look at grace working through holy relationships in the Church. Prayer is evidenced as the fruit of humility and vulnerability in the encounter with our loving, forgiving God. This book is a work of art, expressing the beauty, wisdom and healing of our Orthodox Tradition. Dn. Stephen makes sense of prayer as it relates to the heart, mind and soul and explains it in an accessible and inviting way. Pastors, counselors and Christians seeking God will all benefit from this modern spiritual gem.

—Bp. JOHN (Antiochian Orthodox Bishop of Worcester and New England)

From the very first lines the reader realizes that the book has been written by a heart deeply touched by the grace of God and a mind capable of understanding and organizing fruitfully the inner experience into a sound spiritual order, without reducing the theological dimension to merely human words. Indeed, the writer has attained eloquently a profound presentation of the Philokaliac Tradition on prayer by a fresh, personal and at once ecclesiastical approach, which instantly invites and inspires you to pray.

—Fr. Chrysostom Gr. Tympas, PhD, *Carl Jung and Maximus the Confessor on Psychic Development: The Dynamics Between the 'Psychological' and the 'Spiritual'* Routledge, 2014.

During my youth, there seemed to be little awareness in the Body of Christ of the wisdom and richness of one another's traditions. In these, my older years as a Roman Catholic Sister and spiritual director, I rejoice whole-heartedly and am deeply challenged, as I drink from the wellsprings of the Eastern Orthodox Tradition brought almost poetically into the Twenty-first century for me by the life and writings of Fr. Deacon Stephen Muse.

—Sr. Christine Wiltrakis, MSBT, Blessed Trinity Shrine
Retreat, Ft. Mitchell, AL.

"Thy will be done on earth

As it is in heaven."

ACKNOWLEDGMENTS

G RATEFULLY I WISH to acknowledge the generosity of Bishop Gregory of Nyssa and Hieromonk Ephraim for their labors of love pouring over this manuscript with a fine-tooth comb, and whose suggestions and encouragement have helped significantly to improve it.

I thank also Metropolitan Chrysostomos, Archimandrite Sergius, Fr. Cyprian DuRant, Fr. Panayiotis Papageorgiou, Fr. Vasileios Thermos, Fr. Alexios Trader, Fr. John Stefero, Fr. Harry and Presvytera Kerry Pappas, Sr. Christine Wiltrakis, Fr. Iulian Negru, Bishop John Abdalah, Mother Gabriella, Fr. Chrysostom Tympas, Gerondissa Michaila, and Dr. Chrysostomos Stamoulis, all of whom took precious time to read parts of the manuscript, discuss relevant theological issues and offer their suggestions and encouragement.

Given the nature and importance of prayer in Christian life, whether for monastics or for those living in the world, and my desire to be an authentic witness of the neptic Patristic Tradition, your kindness and honest responses have been a vital ingredient of my willingness to go ahead with publication. I sincerely hope that it will be encouragement for all who read it to make a deeper dive into the embodied life of prayer.

To Fr. Demetrius Nikoloudakis, whose invitation and gentle persistence lured me to Pennsylvania for a prayer retreat, and for those who attended it, I credit you all with having been a catalyst (for the Holy Spirit I hope) for this volume which is built around those three talks I gave for that retreat.

Now with hope in the prayers and intercession of Panaghia, St. Silouan, Elder Sophrony and the choir of all those saints, ascetical fathers and mothers from whose inspired words and hard won wisdom I have benefitted and dared to pluck from their writings and weave into this tapestry, I offer these reflections as a few loaves and fish, to the Lord Jesus Christ, and all those whom He loves, asking for His blessing that we may be nourished according to the measure of the Holy Spirit Who is invisibly at work among us, our Treasure in earthen vessels.

Contents

PREFACE

Prayer is the test of everything; prayer is also the source of everything; prayer is the driving force of everything; prayer is also the director of everything. If prayer is right, everything is right. For prayer will not allow anything to go wrong.

—Saint Theophan the Recluse

THESE OUTWARDLY SIMPLE WORDS of Saint Theophan the Recluse point us to the great mystery and power of prayer. At the same time, they present us, who may not have the experience of this great man of prayer, with many questions: What is prayer? How can it be the source and driving force of everything? How do I know when prayer is right? Who will teach me how to pray?

The book you are holding will not answer these questions, nor will most books, even those written by the most inspired luminaries of the Church. This is not because those texts are in any way flawed, but because any genuine introduction to prayer can only take place through the action of God's grace working with the voluntary action of prayer that each of us personally initiates, in our own time, in our own bodies and in our own circumstances.

In the following pages, Fr. Stephen Muse provides us, not with a manual of prayer, but with an opening into the life of prayer by unveiling for us "the mystery of embodied life and the uncreated divine life." He provides an entranceway for us, as human beings with all our brokenness, weakness and fear, to dialogue with the uncreated life and light of God through prayer. And he invites us into this dialogue through the two complementary parts of this book.

In the first part, Fr. Stephen frames the discussion of prayer and embodied life within three poetic verses of what he calls the "dia-Logos prayer." This prayer, and the chapters which accompany each verse, provide the reader with encouragement and inspiration to enter into a personal dialogue of love with God and with creation. In the second part, we are offered a specific dialogue between Fr. Stephen and a hieromonk; a conversation which immerses us in the wealth of our Orthodox patristic tradition. This is further reflected in the wonderful garden of patristic commentaries, both ancient and contemporary, which follow.

In this patristic garden are a multitude of flowers, each reflecting a unique experience, but all reminding us that, just as Christ Himself was the inspiration for the Holy Fathers, so He serves as our divine inspiration. He is the One who descends into the lower parts of the earth and ascends far above all heavens that he might fill all things with spiritual gifts (Ephesians 4:8–10). Every liturgical hymn of the Church, every writing of the Holy Fathers, and every prayer has one purpose: to take us on this path of descent and ascent with Christ so that we might more fully enter into His life and His love.

This is a daunting task, but this small book is an encouragement for the journey of prayer which both exalts us and humbles us. The wisdom Fr. Stephen offers flows from his own deeply personal experience of this mystery and he points us to a window into our own hearts, not so we can share his experience, but so that we can enter into our own loving relationship with God. How is this to be accomplished? I leave it to the reader to prayerfully partake of the banquet that is set forth in the following pages. In addition, I share the following story from a memorable moment that proved to be a guidepost in my own journey:

On a pilgrimage to the Holy Mountain many years ago, one of the fathers shared with me some wisdom about the will of God. He noted that oftentimes, we are presented with choices and we agonize as we try to discern what the will of God might be. But then this father offered the following paradoxical words: "Sometimes it is not so much a matter of us doing God's will, but of God doing our will." By this, he meant that it is sometimes more productive, not to wait for a divine sign of God's will, which may be slow to come, but to choose one of the paths that lie before us. By persevering in that choice and in patiently confronting the challenges before us, we are doing God's will.

It is the same with prayer. Rather than setting before ourselves the lofty goal of attaining the uncreated light, rather than feeling that we have failed because we have not yet reached unceasing prayer, let us rather joyfully embark on the journey of prayer by offering what we can to the Lord, and also recognizing, as Fr. Stephen reminds us, that "[b]reathing is prayer, but we don't realize it. All the way down to the cellular mitochondria and vital energy of every living being, we *are* prayer."

Everything in this wonderful book provides the reader with an opportunity to learn what it means to truly breathe prayer and invites us to begin and continue the journey of seeking to draw closer to our Lord Jesus Christ with every breath. May all who read it be blessed to discover this for themselves with the help of the Holy Spirit and the prayers of all the Saints.

—His Beatitude Metropolitan Tikhon, Archbishop of Washington, Metropolitan of All America and Canada

INTRODUCTION

I DID NOT SET OUT with intention of writing a book on prayer. Nevertheless in doing so, I have benefited and been further challenged in ways I would not have anticipated. Part I of this volume is edited and expanded from talks given for the general public on Saturday, April 16, 2016, in Wernersville, Pennsylvania, for the 3rd Annual Lenten "Into the Heart of Christ" Prayer Retreat sponsored by St. Matthew's Greek Orthodox Church of Blandon, Pennsylvania on the theme "Prayer and the Embodied Life." Part II is expanded and revised from a letter written in response to a question from an Athonite hieromonk dear to me and who is well-versed in Patristic literature. As such, it includes a significant amount of Patristic references on prayer and a series of extensive quotations selected from among the neptic tradition of the *Philokalia* and contemporary elders related to prayer and embodied life.

I have divided the volume into two parts to reflect these two different audiences, purposes and writing style which have been combined into one book because they are intimately related and together form one whole. Both approach prayer with an understanding that it is an intimate, fully embodied personal response to a love relationship of simplicity and vulnerability with the uncreated God noetically in and through Christ. The effect of this encounter is lived out existentially with one another in this life, and continues after death as uniquely embodied persons. "The body is ontologically the ultimate hypostasis of reality. Paraphrasing G. Florovsky, we can say that in anthropology *the truth without corporeality is a phantom and corporeality without the truth is a cadaver.*"[1]

---

1 Vasiljevic, M. *History, Truth, Holiness: Studies in Theological Ontology and Epistemology,* Alhambra, CA: Sebastian Press, 2011, p. 40.

Most importantly of all, like love, prayer is a gift of God's grace given to the humble, a journey that begins anew at each moment and never allows us to 'arrive' so that we need not humbly begin again and again, as beggars, seeking the Treasure of our Beloved Lord Who has hidden Himself in the last place we would look—yet the only place that can transform us—our own hearts, which are confirmed by embracing Him in each other's. This must never be forgotten. For prayer that does not lead to love of neighbor and all creation is not prayer. It is "this ecstatic love—the offering of ourselves to others—that guides us to finding ourselves."[2] In the sheer silence of the seemingly most forsaken and humble abode of the repentant heart, in a way that passes human understanding, we receive in prayer the One who first welcomes us to life. It is He Who in return, offers the hospitality of forgiveness, love and mercy to every person we meet. Where there is no love, there is no prayer and wherever there is true prayer, love is conceived in the womb of the heart as its first fruit.

Over the past 40 years, both as a clergy and as a pastoral psychotherapist, I have found myself involved in responding to people seeking (knowingly or not) to return to Christ, who had in some way "lost their minds" by being dissociated from their bodies. "Beside themselves," they fell into sin and passions in response to trauma, grief and loss of meaning in life. We all struggle with temptations to avoid reality, seeking relief through imagination in disembodied states. In this way we make "the voluptuous choice" of seeking refuge in the mindless stimulation of our appetites and desires alone because we are unable or unwilling to face reality and trust that God meets us Eucharistically behind and through it all, seeking communion with us in the heart of the very flesh we experience as being the most helpless, empty, forsaken and unlovable. Like prodigal sons and daughters, "it is only if we are able to come to our senses—and this occurs with the help of God—that we ever discover our poverty and nakedness"[3] which is capable of engendering in us true prayer of the heart.

---

    2 Vasileios, A. *The Parable of the Prodigal Son*, Quebec, Canada: Alexander Press, 1996. p. 32.
    3 Ibid. p. 42.

Our contemporary cultural situation is one in which spiritual discontentment is increasingly masked by ideologies of man-made religions (or atheism) of scientism and rational humanism, by the cornucopia of psychological offerings masquerading or set forth as spirituality, and by the distractions of adrenalin-charged virtual reality and the information-dependency created by the media and "digital communities." These monological endeavors have furthered loneliness and increasingly led to self-centered objectification of creation and of each other. The result is that people suffer a great emptiness of heart and meaning that no amount of increased physical vitality, narcotic soothing, acquisition of more "stuff," and immersion in spectacles and "new experiences" can satisfy. I have been, and continue to be, humbled and instructed along the way by contending with my own wounds and temptations in all these areas as well.

As a result of the distortions and tempestuous pace of our overworking, materially comfortable, technology-dependent lives, Christians in Europe and America, increasingly adrift in deracinated post-modern relativity and rational humanism, especially appear to have lost their practical understanding, and consequently their interest, in what the Holy Fathers mean when they say Jesus Christ is both God *and* human and *becomes flesh*[4] for us. In Him two natures, uncreated and created, are seamlessly wed without confusion in one person. The result has been that instead of drinking deeply from the endless noetic well of uncreated divine energies, thousands have been settling for transient emotional enthusiasms generated by technology-enhanced Hollywood style theater churches or they have left the Church to follow religions[5] that offer tangible psychic experiences to fill the void left by materialism but without realizing the depth and breadth of the potential noetic Treasure they have abandoned in the process, one that is capable of bringing the whole creation and every person to life in Eucharistic reciprocity.

---

4 Jn. 1:14.

5 Orthodox Christians do not consider Christianity a religion, but a revelation of God to all humanity. Comparative religion is a form of psychological reductionism that distorts and relativizes this revelation in order to compare it with another.

More and more claim to be 'spiritual' but without interest in "organized religion." There is for many of these seekers, a genuine search for something they find missing from churches whose life seems to be circumscribed by a social, entertainment and business atmosphere in the name of Christ, having "only the form of religion but denying its power"[6] to transform their lives. By contrast, various forms of sought-after meditation, ascetical practices and exotic ritual in other religions are appealing in their ability to provide new experiences which give respite from the banality of ordinary life stripped of the capacity to reveal God's presence. Often this comes at the price of settling merely for experiences of psychic enhancement, emotional stimulation and increased physical vitality in place of finding a real cure for egotism and sanctification of the whole person by the uncreated divine energies in a relationship of love uniting with God, creation, and all humanity.

Others continue their involvement with Church, satisfied with having opportunities to gather, learn and share together what worldly life offers, without realizing that there is an infinite depth to life beyond reason and the senses. Death does not come tomorrow; it is here now, weighing the value of all that we have gathered and all that we *are*. They do not seem to realize that God the Father waits to welcome us, like the prodigal, after we have "come to our senses,"[7] in order to put on the *likeness* of Christ Whose life transfigures our flesh through the uncreated divine energies of the Holy Spirit. Our true life is not synonymous with the confines of time and space, nor is it satisfied by the ever-changing menu of civil religion. Rather, "hid with Christ in God,"[8] our real life is found by tasting the depth of eternal life here and now, which sets in motion the journey of prayer and worship that is fulfilled only after death in a resurrection we cannot achieve by our own human powers alone.

Having been approached repeatedly by those who, like myself, refuse to seek heaven at the price of betraying earth and equally, who do not want to live an earthly life without the blessing of heaven,

---

6 2 Tim. 3:5.
7 "εἰς ἑαυτὸν ἐλθὼν," Lk. 15:17
8 Col. 3:3.

I have gathered some crumbs from the table of the Holy Fathers which have nourished me and added them to my small experience of seeking to live as a married man, father and *papou*, an interior life of watchfulness, repentance and prayer in daily life, over the course of the last forty years. I say forty years, even though I am now 63 years old as I write these words, because it was forty years ago that I discovered *The Philokalia*, the *Way of a Pilgrim*, the Jesus Prayer, and found an experienced guide who helped me discover the value of stilling my body and mind, recollecting my attention, and beginning in a sustained and systematic way to be watchful of the play of thoughts, sensations, imagination and feelings that make up the anatomy of passions influencing the course of my daily life. I must also pay grateful homage to the love and example of my mother, praying beside me on her knees when I was four years old, and suffering a terrible 30-year chronically debilitating illness that ultimately proved fatal, without losing hope in God. Her joy in living and her love for me, were both a vitally important provocation and indispensable preparation for all that came afterward.

I was in seminary when I first discovered the *Writings of the Philokalia*.[9] By then I had already begun searching for a deeper way of prayer that was more than saying words in my head or being satisfied with sentimental devotional feelings or with zealous ideological activism and the new liberation theologies then in vogue, which though valuable, rise no higher than human justice. I didn't want to be a celibate monk. I wanted to marry and live a life of prayer and repentance in the world with a family and children, but with the inner intensity of a hesychast intimately familiar with the unseen world beyond the senses.

St. Niketas Stethatos assures that this can be. "To become a monk does not mean to abandon men and the world, but to renounce the will of the flesh, to be destitute of the passions."[10] The seeming contradiction here dissolves in light of the understanding of those who

---

9   Kadloubovsky, E. and Palmer, G.E.H. (eds.) *Writings from the Philokalia on Prayer of the Heart*, London: Faber & Faber, 1975.

10   Palmer, G.E.H., Sherrard, P., Ware, K. (eds.) *The Philokalia*. Vol. IV, 1995. p. 99.

have tasted and proven this possibility of discovering heaven while living on earth.

Evagrius Ponticus, writing largely to monks, nuns and desert strugglers, declares that "a monk is one who is separated from all and in harmony with all."[11] Then he describes the inward landscape of the heart as the real desert, echoing the words of the Lord regarding the condition needed for the beatific vision.[12] "The intellect becomes a "monk" when it is free of all sins of thoughts, and "perceives" the light of the Holy Trinity at the time of prayer."[13] If repentance and uninterrupted prayer is the goal of monastics and desert dwellers seeking solitude; the whole point of prayer and repentance is to acquire the treasure of the Holy Spirit in a heart of flesh that becomes capable of love. There is nothing about solitude per se that makes it more desirable than life in the world if it does not culminate in this. "It is better to be among thousands with love, then to hide alone in caves with hatred."[14]

The experiences and many conversations with persons that have come across my path since those early beginnings have provided much of the incentive and direction for this small volume. I am certainly no holy elder, nor can I lay claim to being a Patristic scholar nor having seen the uncreated light of the Holy Trinity in a beatific vision. However sincere and longing for God, I remain a dabbler and a dilettante in my life in Christ, a grateful beneficiary of the cloud of witnesses whose struggles and blood have provided encouragement and signposts along the way, giving direction to the small moments of Grace that have provided reassurance and light along the way.

Therefore, I ask forgiveness of the reader for my hubris and inevitable errors and invite and yearn for correction from all who in

---

11 "On Prayer," Cited in Bunge, G. *Dragon's Wine and Angel's Bread: The Teaching of Evagrius Ponticus on Anger and Meekness.* Crestwood, NY: St. Vladimir's Seminary Press, 2009. p. 14.

12 Mt. 5:8.

13 Ibid., p. 14.

14 Kadloubovsky, E. and Palmer, G.E.H. (eds.) *Early Fathers from the Philokalia.* Faber and Faber Limited: London, 1976. p. 115.

humility know the way better than I and by their humility, discernment and compassion may offer wisdom from the Holy Spirit to help me.

—Fr. Dn. Stephen Muse
Feast of the Annunciation
March 25, 2017

PART I

God awards his grace not for work but for humility.
In so far as a person humbles himself, he is visited by Grace.[15]

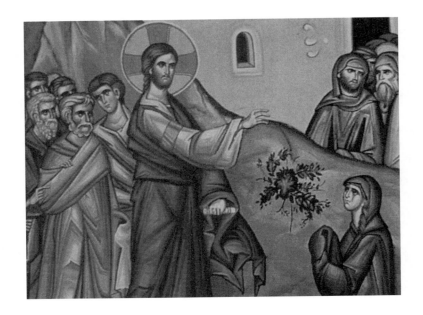

15 John, Fr. *Christ Is In our Midst: Letters from a Russian Monk.* Crestwood, NY:
St. Vladimir's Seminary Press, 1980, p. 4.

Chapter 1

AT THE ALTAR OF THE HEART
BETWEEN HEAVEN AND EARTH

God deserts those engaged in spiritual warfare for three rea-
sons: because of their arrogance, because they censure others,
and because they are so cock-a-hoop about their own virtue.
The presence of any of these vices in the soul prompts God
to withdraw; and until they are expelled and replaced by
radical humility, the soul will not escape just punishment.[1]

—St. Niketas Stethatos

LORD JESUS CHRIST, a word from Your lips can break the heart and a crumb from Your table can heal it forever. Meekness[2] made the Syro-Phoenician woman's[3] prayer bold before You. "The meek [person] does not refrain from love, even if [she] must suffer the worst."[4] St. Gregory Palamas says she "sprang up from the valleys like a sacred lily, exhaling with her words the fragrance of the divine Spirit from her mouth."[5] When she heard You calling her "the lowest of dogs (literally "little dog") in front of your disciples she replied with emphatic self-condemnation and humility, *Truth,*

---

1 Palmer, G.E.H., Sherrard, P., Ware, K. (eds.) *The Philokalia.* Vol. IV, 1995, p. 91.

2 St. Maximus the confessor defines meekness as "courage plus immovability of desire and will" as in the Patristic understanding of Joel 3:10. 'Let the meek become a warrior against evil thoughts and passions.'

3 Mt. 15:27; Mk. 7:24–30.

4 Evagrius Ponticus, cited in Bunge, G. *Dragon's Wine and Angel's Bread.* Crestwood, NY: St. Vladimir's Seminary Press. 2009, p. 82.

5 Veniamin, Christopher (trans.) *Saint Gregory Palamas the Homilies.* Pennsylvania: Mount Thabor Publishing, 2014, p. 340.

Lord (Mt. 15:27)"[6] demonstrating the presence of the Holy Spirit humbly at work in her heart. Humility, contrition, and love made her an example of faith for all Israel. Could Your disciples not see past her ethnicity and 'heterodox' faith in comparison to their imagined superiority as a result of being Your *true* followers? Is that why they scorned her entreaties asking you to "send her away"[7] because she was "crying out after them?" Were they unable to see the Holy Spirit already invisibly at work within her? They never forgot the lesson they learned from her dialogue with You at that moment before you answered her heartfelt prayer and confirmed her faith. They talked about it years later and included it in the Gospel testimony to help us avoid making the same mistake. They understood that all who come after them, will be tempted as they were by similar vainglorious illusions and presumptions of superiority for one reason or another. We are in danger of making the same error whenever we fail to realize Your chosen ones who are messengers of living Tradition are only those who are motivated by love and who in humility persist in the way of the towel and the Cross that You bore for us in the face of all obstacles.

Faith, hope and love for You were woven from the threads of humility in her approach revealing the spiritual unity with You that embraces all humankind in ways that we cannot fully comprehend from surface appearances. Elder Haralambos Dionysiatis recognized the depth of this mother's entreaty as being an example of noetic prayer. He writes that when she

---

6 Ibid., p. 339.

7 Mt. 15:23. The Greek Ἀπόλυσον, (from απολύω) according to Kittel, can be used to mean "release, liberate, forgive" or "dismiss, send away, be rid of." Patristic interpretations vary in viewing the disciples as offering intercession to the Lord to hear her prayer to being annoyed by her shouting or crying after them. Contextually at this point in the narrative, having recently withdrawn from Israel after battling with Pharisees over the exactness of keeping the Tradition of the Elders regarding food, and given the Lord's initial verbal response to this Greek woman, the latter rendering may be more accurate. God's mercy stretches the limits of human comprehension. This is what many of the Pharisees did not appreciate and is something the disciples also had difficulty learning. (cf. Acts 10:12ff), which suggests they may not have been receptive to this foreigner. Many Patristic voices see this as revealing that Christ's ministry is beyond Israel to all who humbly receive Him.

was pleading with Christ over her child, she was saying out loud, "have mercy on me," but with all her soul.
That is prayer of the heart. My child, when the mind is
absorbed in God, even if you pray aloud, the prayer is
called prayer of the heart. It comes from the depths of
the heart. Heart and mind are united with God.[8]

This woman, a foreigner, without the necessary theological or cultural pedigrees to be considered among the Jewish elect, was tested
and revealed by the Lord to be an icon of intercessory noetic prayer
from the heart, born of the Holy Spirit, propelled by love and offered
kneeling before Him in humility and hope. As we approach the subject of prayer it is well to remember we are all in her position whatever our experience, creed and culture.[9] We need her example continually before us showing us the way of humility and love which is
often as hidden from us as Your grace working invisibly in her heart,
was hidden from Your Apostles. From beginning to end, prayer is a
way of love and a path of humility.

Bending low to the ground in love, You have breathed into the
dust and raised us up as living flesh,[10] imprinted with Your Divine
Image and the *potential* to become *persons* in Your *likeness*. It is a
potential, not a guarantee. According to St. Irenaeus (a disciple of St.
Polycarp who had heard the preaching of St. John the Apostle), even

---

8 Monk Joseph. *Abbot Haralambos Dionysiatis, The Teacher of Noetic Prayer*, Athens, Greece: H. Monastery of Dionysiou, p. 214.

9 Gal. 3:28 "There is neither Jew nor Gentile, neither slave nor free, nor is
there male and female, for you are all one in Christ Jesus." This refers to an ontological unity of diversity which cannot be achieved or 'guaranteed' by psychological,
cultural, creedal, biological or philosophical means. Apart from Christ, Who *is* life,
there is no trans-historical or transcultural reality capable of uniting humanity, as
post-modern perspectives have recognized. However, post-modernity rests on the
absolutizing of a philosophical assumption which denies all normative meta-nar-
ratives and is itself incapable of providing a basis for achieving such unity. Only
Christ *is* the trans-historical reality of Life Who is not reducible to creed, culture
or any individual subjective earthly experience. Christ, the Son of God, is "the Way,
the Truth and the Life" (Jn. 14:6) for all, while being irreducible to a philosophical
metanarrative.

10 Vid. Gen. 2:7.

before sin had occurred, humankind was in need of salvation.[11] Why? Because although created in the Image of God, Adam and Eve were spiritually like innocent children, not fully mature. Human nature does not become perfected in the "likeness" of God, automatically, merely by having been created. Spiritual maturity occurs gradually as we encounter Christ, the "first born" and only Lover of humankind through responding to the divine invitation to Communion over a lifetime. When God calls,[12] when Jesus knocks at the door of the heart,[13] *we have to show up.* Something more than deterministic genetics, effort of will, and the maturing of reason is required in response to God's initiative, in order to reach our full human potential. According to the Patristic understanding, *likeness* refers to the virtues inherent to sanctification by the uncreated divine energies of Grace. They are a sign of being in communion with Christ. Achieving the likeness of God is a gift given in response to a long and arduous struggle in faith to obey in body, mind, and soul, the noetic illumination that Christ invisibly communicates to our hearts. Lest we despair of the difficulties faced along this way, St. John Climacus offers a consoling word. "Not everyone can achieve dispassion[14]. But all can be saved and can be reconciled to God."[15]

Encounter with God is made manifest through the paradox of being fully embodied *and* response-able to the uncreated divine energies of Grace simultaneously, not once, but by renewing this intention and inner activity as often as possible over a lifetime. Spiritual maturity, or *sanctification*,[16] arises out of the synergy of "constant col-

---

11   Cf. Panayiotis Nellas, *Deification in Christ.* Crestwood, NY: St. Vladimir's Seminary Press, 1987.

12   Gen 3:9.

13   Rev. 3:20.

14   Dispassion or *apatheia* refers to the freedom from slavery to sin that occurs when one abides in Christ and prays and repents continuously with a pure heart, a rare condition found among very few that culminates in love for others as Christ loves us.

15   Climacus, St. John *The Ladder of Divine Ascent.* Mahwah, NJ: Paulist Press, 1982, p. 240.

16   Often referred to in the Eastern Orthodox Church as "deification"—human by essence, divine by Grace.

laboration with the Holy Trinity's deifying Grace"[17] which gradually opens the door to the illumination of natural contemplation (*theoria*). Union with God (*theosis*),[18] is marked by the willing acceptance of His Cross of love for all the world so that as St. Paul recognized, one can say, "I have been crucified with Christ and it is no longer I but Christ who lives in me."[19] In other words, though we are betrothed to the *Logos* by way of our creation out of nothing, we do not become persons in the likeness of God except by freely responding to the call of God in Christ to have communion with us, to consummate with us at the altar of the heart, the wedding between heaven and earth, whose foundation is Christ Himself.

The journey to human maturity in the *likeness* of God is the journey of love and the path of prayer and embodied presence because Christ Himself unites the uncreated divine essence with creation through fully assuming human nature and being born of a woman. As such, Christianity is a path of spiritual struggle bringing to life the "hidden person of the heart"[20] where this mystery is revealed, involving the whole person in relation to all creation. Jesus declared, "I am the Way, the Truth and the Life. No one comes to the Father except through me."[21] Far more than being merely a romantic, disembodied emotional attachment to the idea of God and an intellectual belief in the existence of a historical Jesus, sanctification involves abiding[22] in the living presence of Jesus Christ on a daily basis. There is only one God and one eternally begotten Son of the Father who unites in His person the fullness of the created order and the uncreated divine essence. There is only One who has revealed love for all the world by risking everything in order to offer us His Own Divinity by protecting our freedom to choose Him without any coercive force

---

17 Larchet, Jean-Claude, *Therapy of Spiritual Illnesses: An Introduction to the Ascetic Tradition of the Orthodox Church*, Montreal, Canada: Alexander Press, 2012.

18 *Theosis* refers to sanctification; to be fully human in essence and fully illumined by the uncreated divine energies as a gift of Grace, united in one person. This is Eucharistic joy.

19 Gal. 2:20.

20 1 Pet. 3:4.

21 Jn.14:6.

22 Jn. 15:4.

whatsoever. He willingly endures whatever it takes to make this possible for us. He is the bridge over which humanity crosses from this world to eternity. In Christ, God is closer to us than our breath and calls us to Himself from our essential being over the entire course of our lifetime. What is our response?

At the heart of the Christian faith is a profound and challenging mystery so simple in its outward manifestation that it is easily overlooked and so unfathomable in its depths that it cannot be comprehended by the rational mind. The eternally begotten Son of God *has become flesh for our sakes and given us His flesh and blood to eat and drink* for the for-giveness[23] of sin and eternal life. God becomes human so that we can finish growing up; so that we can mature from spiritual children with a potential for everlasting life, into beings who fulfill our calling as a royal priesthood, uniting heaven and earth in and through Christ in a perpetual invocation. In humanity, the created order finds a voice and an awareness to commend itself to God in thanksgiving and receives back a blessing that is communicated throughout the entire cosmos. The witness to this holy transformation is the Church. Elder Aimilianos of Simonopetra expresses this beautifully.

> What, then, does it mean, when it says that Christ *spoke to them about the kingdom of God?* It means that He revealed to them the mystery of eternal union between God and man. "I am living," means that "I am living for your sake, for you to have eternal life. When you make me your own, I live in you, and you live in Me." He reveals, in other words, the mystery of the identity between Himself and the Church as His mystical body.
>
> It is as if Christ is saying: "Today I present Myself to you living, but from now on, it will be the kingdom itself, the Church itself, that will render Me present. From

---

23 By using a hyphen I am emphasizing the prevenient aspect of forgiveness which is given by God before we have even sinned. Christ himself is given for us. As Fr. Lev Gillet pointed out, "There was a Cross in the heart of Christ before there was one outside the gates of Jerusalem."

now on, whenever you gather together, you will be My living person and image. *You* are the Church…you cease to be yourselves, and together become Christ."… "I'm searching," He says, "to find the perfect and most natural way of communicating My living presence to you, so that I will be unceasingly in your blood, in your bones, in your flesh." …

We are bound to all those around us, and through them to God, since we are drawn to the invisible by means of the visible… "Go, then, because the two of you are enough. When you gather in My name, when you join together for worship in the life-giving assembly, I live in you, I become you."[24]

This is the path of salvation leading to sanctification. It is a life of liturgical call and response from a unity between the created order and the uncreated divine presence that passes human understanding. In a way we cannot see, in a manner we cannot control, and yet only by our willing assent, we are noetically re-created in love from Image to likeness and *become ourselves.* Why? Because we are loved into being by One who loves beyond measure and offers us His life as our own. He does not assimilate or obliterate us in this union, but we are completed and discover the mystery of being-in-communion with Christ while remaining uniquely ourselves, body, soul and spirit and in relation to the whole of Creation. In this action we are one with all humanity, each one being an "otherness in communion"[25] with all the rest.

Fear of the immensity of this unmerited gift, even though desired above all else, is the beginning of wisdom[26]. Humility and awe before

24 Archimandrite Aimilianos, (trans. Nicholas Constas), *The Way of the Spirit,* Athens, Greece: Indiktos, 2009. pp. 184–186.
25 Vid. Zizioulas, J. *Communion and Otherness: Further Studies in Personhood and the Church,* New York: Bloomsbury T & T Clark, 2007 and *Being as Communion: Studies in Personhood and the Church.* New York: St. Vladimir's Seminary Press, 1997.
26 Psalm 111:10; Proverbs 9:10, "The Fear of the Lord is the beginning of wisdom" refers to awe, wonder and recognition of the Holiness of God before Whom "all mortal flesh keeps silent." This distinction between creature and the Holy Other of the Creator determines how we enter into prayer and a different kind of embodied

awareness of our incarnation, suspended on the Cross between
non-being and the abyss of death that separates mortal flesh from
the divine Presence, is the mother of repentance. This is the condition of spiritual sobriety from which the cry of noetic prayer arises,
seeking re-union with our Creator who becomes flesh for us, which
is the seedbed of love. Our flesh, our will, our actions, become His.
We are clothed with the vestments of divine Grace. The embodied
life of prayerful presence is bread for the journey of becoming fully
human.

Both the invisible divine life and the visible creation flow toward
us constantly like a moving highway and we find ourselves going
forward in response to the continual gifts of God pouring through us.
It is because Christ is seeking us that we begin to consciously search
for Him. Let us then learn from the Syro-Phoenician woman, and
bowing low in humility before all obstacles, urged on by love and
intercession, search to discover Him in the place of the heart where
we have abandoned the world[27], the opinion of others and even ourselves, for love of Him. From this a strange paradox is revealed as St.
Isaac the Syrian observed, "Be contemptible in your own eyes, and
you will see the glory of God in yourself."[28] St. Symeon the New
Theologian expressed the same. "To have faith is to die for Christ
and for His commandments; to believe that this death brings life; to
regard poverty as wealth, and lowliness and humiliation as true glory
and honor; to believe that by not possessing anything one possesses
everything."[29] When our hands and minds let go of serving all lesser

life. Christ unites the created order and the uncreated in Himself. He is the "door"
through which we enter into prayer, worship and the sanctified, embodied life.

27 By "world" is meant the passions which consist of attachment to pleasure
and pain, like and dislike that are at the heart of the suffering that arises when, out
of pride and presumption we grasp at (and are grasped by) created life without
having first in thanksgiving, offered it back to God for blessing. Worldliness is the
rejection of Eucharistic life and a denial of our ontological origins in the Image and
likeness of One beyond this world.

28 St. Isaac the Syrian, *The Ascetical Homilies of St. Isaac the Syrian* revised second edition. Trans. From the Greek and Syriac, Holy Transfiguration Monastery,
Boston, MA, 2011. p. 165.

29 Palmer, G.E.H., Sherrard, P., Ware, K. (eds.) *The Philokalia*. Vol. IV, 1995,
p. 25.

desires, our hearts are filled by the Greatest One. "Blessed are the pure in heart, for they shall see God."[30]

30　Mt. 5:8.

Chapter 2

BREATHE IN GOD, BREATHE OUT LOVE

It is proper for a Christian even when he has done all he is commanded to do, all righteousness, to consider that he has done nothing. The man who has laid hold of the truth is truly humble. He does not judge other men.[31]

—St Macarius of Egypt

WHEN IT COMES TO PRAYER, humility is the only sure starting place, and love is the only sign of mature fruit. Prayer is basic to life, even a necessity. Yet it is easily missed in our efforts to discover something spectacular. Thankfully, difficulties arise to awaken us from our dreams and bring us back to earth where the way begins right at the doorstop of our ordinary lives. It is in our hearts that we must face a world we too quickly take for granted and "light the fire in us with tears and struggle."[32] The struggle to remain present to our life and to Christ at the same time, to receive all and everyone in it as a testimony to God's invisible presence, "everywhere and in all places" is the paradoxical essence of prayer. A theologian is one who prays and prays truly only if prayer becomes flesh in love manifested in everyday life.

A former kindergarten teacher said in a lecture to an auditorium full of pastoral counselors, "We breathe in God and breathe out love. It's that simple." Breathing is prayer, but we don't realize it. All the way down to the cellular mitochondria and vital energy of every living being, we *are* prayer. We are pulsing with energy and movement, life becoming aware of itself in search of its origin. We are creatures

31 Epistle of St. Macarius, *The Ascetical Homilies of St. Isaac the Syrian* revised second edition. Trans. From the Greek and Syriac, Holy Transfiguration Monastery, Boston, MA, 2011, p. 565, 567.

32 St. Syncletica, *Sayings of the Desert Fathers* cited in Clement, O. *The Roots of Christian Mysticism: Texts from the Patristic Era with Commentary,* New York: New City Press. 1993. p. 231.

made in the Image of God, a royal priesthood, invited to participate in a perpetual *anaphora*[33] at the altar of the heart, vested with a potential for lifting up all creation in our hearts, gratefully offering back to God everything that has been given, before we receive it back with the one essential ingredient that proves transformative. It is the most *human* element of all, the bread for our being—our conscious thanksgiving—our *Eucharist*[34] which points us toward God found in the heart of flesh. Elder Aimilianos writes,

> We no longer search for God outside of ourselves, because now He emerges from within us, from the innermost shrine of the soul within the temple of the body. Christ has taken up his abode within us, and He is inseparably united to the Father and the Holy Spirit. Paradise, then, is not a place that we seek somewhere outside of ourselves, but rather within ourselves, because each of us has become an intimate part of it, *like precious stones built into a spiritual house* (1 Pet. 2.5).[35]

Receiving the Eucharist "worthily"[36] involves much more than merely swallowing bread and wine. Human development, far from being an automatic unfolding biological and psychological process of satisfaction of appetites, enculturation, procreation and inventing things, has to do with becoming aware of the Author of life, not just intellectually, but ontologically in the heart from "above"[37] and responding existentially to the world from the impact of the encounter. In the midst of the struggle between this created world and our intimations of the invisible uncreated divine life, we make

---

33   From the Greek (ἀναφορά) which refers to the priest's offering up to God the gifts of bread and wine for consecration. This action and moment are the heart of the Divine Liturgy in the Orthodox Church where the celebrant invokes the Holy Spirit to change the bread and wine into the Body and Blood of Christ.

34   The word Eucharist comes from the Greek root related to thankfulness.

35   Aimilianos, A. *The Way of the Spirit: Reflections on Life in God.* Greece: Indiktos, 2009. p. 349.

36   Cf. 1 Cor. 11:27–30.

37   Jn. 3:3 this is a translation from a Greek word ἄνωθεν that here carries the meaning of being born from noetic encounter with the uncreated divine energies of the person of God.

our choices a thousand times a day. "I set before you this day, blessing and curse, life and death, therefore choose life so that you and your descendants may live,"[38] says the Lord. In all that we do, we either seek "Thy will be done on earth" or we do not. Either way, whether known or unknown, it remains true that I *am* only because *Thou art* and this entails a privilege along with an enormous potential for response-ability.

Cursed is the man or woman who does not realize this. The Tempter denies humanity the possibility of deliberately living between the two worlds and being inheritors of the eternal kingdom responding continually to God. He suggests instead, as with Adam and Eve in the Garden,[39] that human beings find their fulfillment and divine destiny to be "like gods" monologically through self-will, pleasure, and imagination. He suggests we hold our breath; disrupt the liturgy of continual flow between earth and heaven, which results in the blindness of experiencing ourselves as being fully determined by appetite, biological hunger and reason – "men without chests" as C. S. Lewis colorfully described our heartless fallen condition. Jesus responded to this temptation by saying, "Man does not live by bread alone,"[40] but only from the life that arises through Communion with the Holy Other. Breathing is life, not something we do once and a while when we feel like it. No one breathes "occasionally." It is simple; we breathe or die.

The response God seeks from humanity is not merely a determined one from the fact of our having been created, but as Nicholas Loudovikos explains, commenting on the theology of St. Maximos the Confessor, God seeks "an answering *dia-logos*, or dialogue, expressed, on the part of the creature, as a *natural will*, which is nothing other than the response of the creature to the invitatory attraction that God exerts upon it through his *logos*/will."[41] In other

---

38 Deut. 11:26.

39 Vid. Gen. chapter 3.

40 Mt. 4:4.

41 Loudovikos, N, *Hell and Heaven, Nature and Person. C. Yannaras, D. Stăniloae and Maximus the Confessor on Holiness: The Sacrament of Surprise, International Journal of Orthodox Theology* 5:1 (2014) urn:nbn:de:0276–2014–1027, p. 17.

words, our personal response to the uncreated divine life over a life-time, is what completes our formation in the divine likeness. In this way, the divine will is expressed through creation itself from the heart of humankind, illumining and transforming both in the process. Fr. Dumitru Staniloae points to the reciprocal nature of this exchange which truly spiritualizes the world rather than desacralizes it as a commodity.

> God freely creates the world to make it spiritual and transparent for himself... through the agency of man inasmuch as it is through man that God inserted free spirit within the world. Through the human spirit inserted within the world, the divine Spirit is Himself at work to bring about the spiritualization of the world through His operation within the soul of man, and in a special way, through His incarnation as man.[42]

The breath of God creates humankind, but it is Jesus Christ, the *Logos*-become-Eucharist Who is the true food of man's being. Knowledge derived from encounter with God transforms us. Apart from this nourishment we are not yet fully alive, but deaf, dumb, blind, paralyzed and demonically possessed as depicted in the Gospels, while thinking in our naiveté and pride, that we are already enlightened and free to do whatever we want. This upside-down attitude is because we have not begun to repent. The renewal of our darkened minds and the replacing of our hardened hearts of stone with a heart of flesh has not yet begun. Something else is needed from us than intellectual assent or even emotional zeal, and that is *Communion with the Holy*. We cannot find this simply by gathering information from reading books or merely by ascetical bodily labors. Communion involves the risk of personal encounter and all that is entailed by an authentic receptive meeting with another.

> The believer, who moves within the territory of super-natural knowledge, the "knowledge" of the Uncreated,

---

42 Staniloae, D. *The Experience of God: Orthodox Dogmatic Theology, Vol. II. The World: Creation and Deification*, Brookline, MA: Holy Cross Orthodox Press, p. 81.

is not called upon to learn something metaphysically, or to accept it logically, *but to "undergo" something, by communing with it.* [emphasis added].[43]

No one can look upon God the Father's face (essence) and survive. But confronted with the condescension of God in the face of the Risen Christ through the Holy Spirit, I begin to comprehend that I am not merely a sinner, but cut apart from Him I have no life in myself. Except for God's invitation to life, I am a non-being. "Fear of God is the beginning of wisdom."[44] Repentance is ultimately the dawning recognition of the infinite abyss that separates me from God. Or as St. Isaac the Syrian put it, "Whoever knows himself" in this way "is greater than one who raises the dead." Speaking in parables, Jesus said the same in a different way. "When you have done everything you were supposed to do..." when you arrive at that moment of facing the living God, "say I am an unworthy servant."[45] This simple statement confounds pride and reorients us to the dialogical reciprocity of our Eucharistic relationship. It is perplexing, even disappointing and depressing to our creaturely presumptions in proportion to the self-reliance and presumption of autonomy that arises from our failure to approach God at the edge of human self-sufficiency. We were not created to be alone. "Man defined by himself, independently of his relation to God that is inscribed in his very nature, is a non-human-being. There is no such thing as pure human nature; man is man-god, or else he does not exist."[46] Humility of the most extreme kind is the only possible avenue by which to approach God and even this is possible only in Christ Himself who is the perfect humility and condescension of God. Christ empties Himself in order to fill us with His life. Elder Arsenie Papacioc, one

---

43   Metallinos, G. *The Way: An Introduction to the Christian Faith.* From Chapter 11 "Faith and Science as a Theological Problem, http://impantokratoros.gr/6072C7D8.en.aspx, downloaded 1–18–2016.

44   Prov. 9:10.

45   cf. Lk. 17:10.

46   Larchet, Jean Claude, *Therapy of Spiritual Illnesses: An Introduction to the Ascetic Tradition of the Orthodox Church.* (Kilian Sprecher, trans.) Vol. 1, Alexander Press: Montreal, 2012. p. 26

of the most revered Romanian elders of our time, pointed out that "humility is genuine only when Christ is present."[47] This is true for all the virtues because Christ *is our life*. This is why St. Paul can say, "It is no longer I but Christ who lives in me."[48]

When the film of pride and the sleep of self-contentedness is wiped from the eye of my heart, I know I am but dust called by the Divine breath into life. Made in the Image of God, there is in me, the possibility of being born "from above"[49] from beyond this world and entering into real life. Eternal life is a gift and a potential; never a certainty or a guarantee. God is ever offering Himself to us in hopes that we are willing to undergo the process of responding to the potentials that are opened up through Communion with Him. *We cannot be saved without our consent.*[50] In Christ God has proposed marriage with humanity purely from love and waits for our response. We are unique creatures invited to taste the eternal Eucharistic joy of never being complete in and of ourselves alone, but only in response to breathing in the divine Grace and breathing out life and gratefulness beyond words. We are made for love and communion with God.

The path to becoming ourselves, becoming persons in the *likeness* of Jesus Christ, is the most precious gift of all; the freedom to be loved and to love. Theology is love that derives from worship and calls for more prayer in and endless circle. The divine breath becomes flesh in our lives through our free obedience and this leads to greater love which transforms our relationship with others through our bodies through communion.

---

47 Archimandrite Arsenie (Papacioc) "Eternity Hidden in the Moment" The Orthodox Word. (St. Herman of Alaska: California, 2011) No. 281, p. 289.

48 Gal. 2:20.

49 In Jn. 3:3 Jesus tells Nicodemus, "You cannot see the Kingdom of God unless you are born "from above" (ἄνωθεν) that here carries the meaning of being born from a noetic encounter with the uncreated divine energies of the person of God that is beyond human reasoning.

50 While God does not violate human freedom which is essential to the personal hypostasis in the Image of God, nevertheless, God's mercy and love suffice for infants and persons who are without adequate mental capacity to assent. Divine Grace is a mystery beyond human comprehension alluded to in one of the prayers of St. John of Damascus which includes the fervent petition: "Whether I will it or not, save me." (http://stbasilthegreat.org/resources/prayers/evening-prayers/).

> In essence my body is my relationship to the world, to others, it is my life as communion and as mutual relationship. Without exception, everything in the body, in the human organism, is created for this relationship, for this communion, for this coming out of oneself. It is not an accident, of course that love, the highest form of communion, finds its incarnation in the body; the body is that which sees, hears, feels, and thereby leads me out of the isolation of my I.[51]

To those who receive what is given and live it out existentially in obedient response to love, still more is given. It is indeed simple, but not at all an easy journey.

Christian faith is not an armchair philosophy. We don't receive a "get out of hell free" card by simply assenting to the historical existence of Jesus or by arguing the case for salvation by Grace in some kind of imaginary judicial courtroom using Scripture quotations as our evidence, while living our life exactly the same as before. Salvation is acquisition of the Holy Spirit Whose presence is revealed in passion-bearing prayer, love for others and for the entire creation. From the struggle to pray and to love we slowly enter deeper and deeper into the depths of repentance. We receive the overwhelming repeated gift of forgiveness and the oil of mercy begins to flow from a crushed and humbled heart offering itself for the life of the world just as Christ does. Apart from this kind of healing myrrh that flows from the heartbreak of struggle and repentance that slowly replaces the heart of stone with the heart of flesh that is Christ Himself, any words about prayer or instructions in Christian life are misguided or incomplete. We are embodied creatures. We are called to life in the flesh and it is a heart of flesh that experiences the struggle with the Spirit that transforms us into the likeness of Christ Who is the Bridegroom of our souls and bodies. We become response-able for the gift of life, by living the words of the prayer Jesus taught his disciples, "Thy will be done on earth as in heaven."

---

51 Schmemann, A. *O Death, Where Is Thy Sting?* Crestwood, NY: St. Vladimir's Seminary Press, 2003, p. 42.

With this in mind, as we turn to discuss the subject of prayer, let me offer two caveats to everything I am going to say. The first is illustrated by a story I came across many years ago.[52] It happens that a monk was on a desert journey between monasteries when he happened upon an old farmer pouring milk out of a bucket on to a rock at the edge of the desert. Puzzled, he asked the farmer why he was wasting his milk like that.

"Oh no," said the farmer. "It's not a waste at all. I have been doing this every morning for over a decade. It gives me great joy to take the first fruits of the milking and offer it to the Lord. You see, I pour it into a small cleft in the rock and by the evening when I come back here to say my prayers, it is always gone. It has been this way for me for as long as I have had my cows. I have been blessed."

The monk smiled and shook his head sadly and explained to the farmer, "The Holy Gospels tell us that "God is Spirit." He doesn't drink milk. "And those who would worship Him, must worship in spirit and in truth."[53]

The old farmer, who could not read, but had great respect of monks and for the Holy Scriptures, listened carefully and decided he would go and see for himself. The next morning, after he had poured out the milk, the farmer stood some ways off behind a tree and watched as three little foxes followed their mother out from their den under the rock and lapped it up. Humbled by what he saw, and disappointed, the old farmer picked up the bowl and returned to his home very thoughtful.

Meanwhile the monk continued on his way, stopping occasionally to read from spiritual writings, grateful that he could read, and continuing on his journey repeating his prayers as he was accustomed. After a few days, he heard a familiar voice in the silence. "Yes Lord, what is it?"

"Father, you are right. I am Spirit and I don't drink milk. But you are so, so wrong. Now all my little foxes are starving and the farmer is despondent because he no longer knows how to worship Me."

---

52   A version of this old tale can be found in Tikhon, A. *Everyday Saints and Other Stories*, Moscow, Russia: Pokrov Publications, 2012, p. 209.

53   Jn. 4:24.

Presuming to judge and instruct others in matters of the heart without first gaining sufficient understanding of their unique circumstances is a recipe for disaster. Careful listening and compassionate interest in someone are children of the humility arising from repentance in the face of one's own repeated failures and human weakness. He who has born all human suffering and helplessness unto death has shown the greatest interest. He alone comprehends humankind sufficient to instruct and to judge and his mercy endures forever.

Whatever I say about prayer I don't want it to have the effect that the monk had on the farmer. We must remember that the Holy Spirit brings us to worship in ways that might be surprising and to separate the tares from the wheat is something for a discerning spiritual guide to help with, and for the angels at the bidding of the Holy Spirit. This is not an excuse to do any old thing we want, but rather a caveat to remind us that it is only the Holy Spirit in a guileless heart of faith that can show us how to pray. This too is love and wherever love accompanies faith, the way is easy. It is true that there are many good instructions for preparing the way for prayer. These include psalmody, the historical prayers of the Church, prostrations, fasting, stillness, collected attention, and so on. Trying everything all at once can be overwhelming and lead to spiritual indigestion. Absent a good spiritual father or mother to guide, each one must make the effort that is called for in his or her life, never forgetting that the essence of it all remains love and not that we love God but the faith that God first loves us.[54] St. Porphyrios encourages us in this way when he says, "You don't need to put effort into prayer when you have divine love. What's important is not the duration of prayer but the intensity (of devotion). Prayer even for just five minutes given to God with love and yearning may be superior to one who prays all night (without it). It's a mystery but that's the way it is."[55]

The second story I want us to have in mind as we begin to think about prayer, happened when I was in Greece and visited Karea, a

---

54 I Jn. 4:10.

55 St. Porphyrios. *Life and Words* (Greek) Trans. Holy Monastery of Pantokrator, Holy Monastery of Chrisopigi of Chania, 2003. http://www.impantokratoros.gr/melancholy-sadness-anxiety.en.aspx.

women's monastery in Athens. I had an opportunity to talk with Mother Philothei and at one point I was asking her, "What is this action we are responsible for as human beings in prayer?" Gently pressing her from every direction, I was trying to get a very specific, concrete and practical response. She said something I had heard many, many times but this time it slipped into my heart and I began to well up with tears. "He comes *to us*." she said. Of course! *He comes to us*… What a revelation and reversal of my focus on the importance of my own actions instead of gratefulness for God's! Her response was like a glass of cool water splashed in some weary place of my heart that received it immediately beneath my intellectual awareness as I continued pressing the question.

"But Mother, even if He comes to us and knocks at the door of our hearts, what is the action I am responsible for to open the door?" With simplicity and gentle sweetness, she said something even more beautiful and arresting to me; something that once again reoriented me to a necessary, yet elusive, direction in pursuit of any and all ascetical efforts and certainly for prayer. She said, "We must become as the thief on the Cross, so that after the doors of heaven are shut, we blow underneath with the dust." Humility again. My heart opened like a bloom to the Grace pouring through her gentle words with more tears. Gratefulness and peace, for a moment, eased the weight of my own egotism and self-preoccupation, which was gently exposed to me once again.

Let us keep the wisdom of these two stories in mind, along with the Syro-Phoenician woman, as a frame, which fixes prayer like a precious stone at the heart of a setting of humility and love. Humility is a sign of Christ's presence. The same is true of love and all the virtues. Alone we can do nothing, but we are privileged to enter into life through Christ and when we do, we may be swept under the door, sheared like lambs by the Lord's humility, of all the possessions that have accumulated over years of our attempts to find our way by our own efforts alone. Like the rich young ruler, struggling to make our way into eternal life on our own power of accomplishment and asking what more we should be doing, Christ looks upon us with love and hopes that we will take the leap of faith that changes everything.

"If you would be perfect[56], then sell all your possessions and come and follow me."[57] In other words, let go of your self-sufficiency, vainglory and personal accomplishments and live freely as I do, receiving whatever God the Father offers in the moment, gratefully without asking for more. We may even put milk on a rock and out of ignorance make our offerings and worship in ways that depart from the correctness of Holy Tradition, but still be swept under the door because of the mercy and goodness of the Lord who seeks out the lost, who receives the most unlikely gifts of children and who invites those most hopeless and bereft in this world to a seat at the table of His heart.

We can take comfort that the humility of Christ is so great that He comes wherever we are and takes whatever we offer, our five loaves and fishes, and makes it into a banquet of salvation. He prepares a table for us in the presence of our enemies and anoints our head with oil[58] until our hearts are overflowing. No matter where we are or what we are involved in, we need but turn to Him and He will respond. "God judges our repentance not by our efforts but by our humility."[59]

So dear reader, with this preamble in mind, forgive me for presuming to speak on this topic of prayer and may God protect you from making prayer anything other than a sigh from the heart in faith, hope, and love leading to a repentance so profound that St. Paul can say, "It is no longer I but Christ who lives in me." and "I can do all things through Christ Who strengthens me."[60] For Christ is our life and pays attention to the slightest sighs of our hearts that are prompted by love for Him.

---

56 The Greek word τέλειοι translated as "perfect" means "complete" – to "hit the mark" of becoming in the likeness of God as the unique being God created each of us.

57 Mt. 19:21.

58 From Psalm 23.

59 St. John Climacus, *The Ladder of Divine Ascent*, Mahwah: NJ: Paulist Press, Step 26, p. 138.

60 Phil. 4:13.

Chapter 3

LORD, LOVE THE WORLD
THROUGH ME

If someone only wants to pray when he is attending God's Church, and has no concern at all for prayer at home, in the streets or in the fields, then even when he is present in church he is not really praying.[61]

—St. Gregory Palamas

THE FEARFUL AND WONDROUS PREDICAMENT we human beings find ourselves in is that flesh and blood wrestle with uncreated divine life. God recreates us by taking our flesh as His own, uniting it to His divinity. There are two distinct natures, created and uncreated, held together in the person of Jesus Christ, seamlessly yet without confusion. The joining of divinity and created human life in Christ opens up the possibility for our transformation by cooperation with the invisible divine energies of Grace.

At the heart of Christian faith is a mystery of the joining of embodied life and the uncreated divine life.

> Christianity speaks about the restoration of life as communion, it speaks about the spiritual body that over the course of our whole life we have developed through love, through our pursuits, through our relationships, through our coming out of ourselves. It speaks not about the eternity of matter, but about its final spiritualization; about the world that finally becomes truly a body—the life and love of mankind; about *the world that has become fully communion with Life* [emphasis added].[62]

---

61 *Saint Gregory Palamas the Homilies.* (Trans.) Christopher Veniamin. Mount Thabor Publishing: Pennsylvania. 2014, Homily 7.

62 Schmemann, A. *O Death Where is Thy Sting?* Crestwood, NY: St. Vladimir's

St. Gregory Palamas likens the divine energies of Grace to the warm light of the sun that reaches us from afar, being one with the sun itself, and yet felt by us. Christ makes it possible for us to re-member and abide in Him through receiving bread and wine as His own body and blood. Our fervent prayer is that we learn through this not to approach bread and wine as mere food without awareness but that it conveys also the miracle of Christ's own presence. We want to approach the Chalice with fear of God, with faith in what our senses cannot reveal to us and with love that hopes, believes and endures all things for the surpassing worth of being loved by Jesus Christ.

Incarnation, death and resurrection, like the bread and wine of Eucharist, are all earthy, embodied events transformed and illumined noetically by invisible uncreated divine energy. The *Logos* who is God, dwells among us and reveals His glory in the flesh by making it possible to receive Him in the bread and the wine. He invites us as we turn around, to regard the world and everyone in it with the eyes of our hearts, illumined by Grace so that we begin to realize all heaven and earth declare the glory of God.

According to Orthodox theology, the entire human being—both soul and body—is to be saved and deified. Fr. John Romanides wrote that *theosis,* or illumination by Grace,

> is not something that only the human rational faculty experiences. During the experience of *theosis,* the entire person participates in this experience. Even the body participates with all its senses in normal working order. When someone sees Christ in glory, that person is completely alert. So this person does not merely see something in his mind. He sees with his body as well.[63]

This is why I suggested the title of these talks as "Treasure in Earthen Vessels: Prayer and the Embodied Life." Because this intercourse between uncreated noetic divine life and the created world

---

Seminary Press, 2003, pp. 43–44.

63   *Patristic Theology,* Fr. John Romanides, Thessaloniki: Greece, Uncut Mountain Press, 2008, p. 74.

that occurs, *dia-Logos*[64] in and through Christ, finds its fulfillment at the altar of the human heart which is the place of greatest struggle. "Divine Grace cannot actualize the illumination of spiritual knowledge unless there is a natural faculty capable of receiving the illumination. But that faculty itself cannot actualize the illumination without the Grace which God bestows."[65] Both God and the personal heart must consent to the marriage between heaven and earth which is born out of the synergy between our human freedom and powers and the uncreated Divine energies which purify soul and body and give birth to the "hidden person of the heart."[66] However arduous the struggle of prayer, we must remember that "God is love"[67] and from beginning to end, "the mystery of salvation belongs to those who choose it, not to those who are compelled by force."[68]

I divided the talks into three sections following three lines from what I call the *dia-Logos* prayer:

> *Lord, love the world through me.*
> *Let me love the world through You.*
> *And be loved by You through the world.*

All three of these petitions together for me capture the harmony of a fully-embodied, Eucharistic, Trinitarian life. They are a spiritual plumb line orienting me to life lived in and through Christ. Beginning with "Lord, love the world through me," there is the recognition that human beings are first of all stewards of creation. We are emissaries of the Logos, a royal priesthood with a very specific vocation. St. Athanasius captured this in his oft-quoted summary of

---

64 *dia-Logos*, literally "through the Logos" refers to the encounter between God and persons that occurs at the altar of the heart in love that proves transformative because of the noetic illumination from Christ's presence "wherever two or more are gathered in His name." Cf. Muse, S. *When The Heart Becomes Flame: An Eastern Orthodox Approach to the dia-Logos of Pastoral Counseling, 2nd edition* and *Being Bread*, Waymart, PA: St. Tikhon's Monastery Press, 2015.

65 St. Maximos the Confessor, *The Philokalia, Vol II*, Fourth Century on Various Texts 12, p. 238.

66 1 Pet. 3:4.

67 1 Jn. 4:8.

68 St. Maximos the Confessor, *The Philokalia*, On the Lord's Prayer, p. 289.

the heart of Orthodox theology when he said, "God became man so that man could become God." I believe it was Romanian theologian, Fr. Dumitru Staniloae who added a second part, which is stunning, equally true and revelatory, completing the theological circle. "God became man so that man could become human."[69]

This is a very rich extrapolation: *God became human so that we can become human.* The *Logos* has proposed to us and waits for our response. We cannot fulfill our human vocation until we choose how we shall respond. It is not just that the Logos creates us and leaves us on a rock in space trying to grow up. The Logos suffers with us. He unites the created conditions of our existence in order to save and complete us. He is a passion-bearer from the beginning to the end. He offers His life as our own. He knows we are not going to be able to make a proper response to such an unfathomable gift until we begin to learn from Him through our struggles, little by little, what it means. This is the challenge of a lifetime and we are going to be stretched, roughed up and like the Apostle Peter, "taken where you do not want to go."[70]

From the very beginning, Christ is here, right in the middle of everything. It is extraordinarily important to realize that the Cross is the Tree of Life and exists not because we are bad boys and girls so that Jesus has to be punished as an atonement for our sins to appease an angry God. The Cross is the Father's willingness to take the risk of suffering and death for His creation to open up the possibility that we become persons capable of loving Him (and one another and all creation) in return as He loves us. The Cross is also hidden in a mother's love who, with a child in her womb, when she gets sick and it hurts and she is stressed, reconfigures every movement as a reminder of carrying the divine life and so she willingly and joyfully bears it. Christ's yoke is the easiest of all, even though He carries the heaviest burden, because He loves completely and is pregnant

---

69   Recalled during the talk I gave, but I have been unable to locate the citation for this. The closest in meaning I have found is a citation in Ware. K. *The Orthodox Way,* Crestwood, NY: St. Vladimir's Seminary Press, p. 87 "The glory to which man is called is that he should grow more godlike by growing ever more human."

70   Jn. 21:18.

with creation. How can this be? We are worn down by all sorts of things and Christ says "Come to me all you who are heavy-laden and burdened and I will give you rest."[71] Why? Because He loves us. He *is* love. Love pays any price. Love creates the world and then goes to hell if necessary for the sake of the beloved. So here is an amazing creative process that God not only gives life creating us out of nothing, but also supports the spiritual gestation and gradual development of the lives of His children at great cost to Himself, until we blow under the door like the thief on the Cross.

Praying for Christ to love the world through me is a prayer that the Lord might remove the stone of vainglorious self-love from my heart and bring life to the person whose heart is hid with Christ in God, Who becomes flesh and dwells among us full of Grace and truth. It is only the heart of flesh that is broken for love and through repentance tastes the sweet Grace of Christ's love, mercy and humility that can receive the Holy Spirit. The vainglorious self-loving heart of stone has only contempt for humanity as it ruthlessly seeks its owns self-perfecting. Anything less than the perfection of God is disgusting. The heart of stone is the spirit of criticism. It is the gaze of Lucifer, the Medusa, offering the devil's food of desire for perfection that serves personal glory rather than offers itself to God and suffers for the sake of the other.

By contrast, Christ our God has a heart of flesh that weeps over Jerusalem, at Lazarus' grave and is broken a thousand times for love of God's children. He looks upon the world with mercy and compassion and never with contempt. He is ever willing to go to hell for those He loves, undergoing every suffering of every creature in all times and places. "As you have done unto the least of these you have done unto Me."[72]

Why does Christ do this? As the *Logos*, St. John tells us, every aspect of creation that was made, was made through Him. The Son created the whole cosmos and loves the world so much that He chose to condescend to be born a human being, rendering conception itself a holy event. He took on the whole of human life in its entirety, from

---

71 Mt. 11:28.
72 Mt. 25:40.

birth to death, opening up the possibility of divinizing every aspect of human development. Unlike Lucifer who has contempt for the created order because of the obvious imperfections of creation when compared to the uncreated God, Christ was born of a human mother and entrusted Himself to her.

As an infant, He drew milk from his mother's breasts and warmth from her arms. Her skin soothed him[73]. Her voice was music to His ears, as with any child and mother. We can easily underestimate the importance of the capacity of sensual interactions between the mother and the newborn as being expressive of the purity of heart which provides theological lessons before spoken language is understood. The mother's embodied responsiveness to her child's face and need for mirroring, was as essential to Jesus as it is to every human child. When we underestimate this dimension of the early mother-child attachment at the human and biological levels we betray the unity of "two natures unconfused"[74] inadvertently laying the groundwork for a misguided asceticism. It is the disharmonizing effect of sinful passions that we struggle to overcome, not the body itself or its natural rhythms, which are capable of participating in and expressing the sanctification of the whole person in an organic way. Both Christ and the Holy Theotokos exemplify this—Christ by essence, and the Holy Theotokos by Grace, through her willing surrender to the divine will.

St. Gregory Palamas, defender of the monastic hesychasts of Mt. Athos saw the Holy Theotokos as the epitome of *hesychia* or stillness.[75] The hallmark of the life of prayer according to the holy neptic fathers of the *Philokalia* is stillness. Let all mortal flesh keep silence before that which goes beyond it! No words. She is an ascetic par excellence and a paradigm of *nepsis* or watchfulness. Her whole life

---

73 We see this tenderness expressed in icons known as the "sweet kissing" which show Christ cheek to cheek in his mother's arms.

74 The dogma of Christ's fully human nature and fully uncreated divine nature united unconfusedly in one person, even as a developing infant, forms an organic unity with the Holy Theotokos' sanctified human nature (by union with the divine energies) expressed in her fully human maternal presence.

75 Vid. Veniamin, Christopher (trans.) *Saint Gregory Palamas the Homilies.* Pennsylvania: Mount Thabor Publishing, 2014. Homily 53.

is one of embodied prayer while living in the world of family, community and the daily affairs of ordinary life. While doing all these things she inwardly ponders the deeper spiritual meanings of events that are revealed ontologically only by an intimate encounter in the flesh[76] with the noetic uncreated order of divine Grace.

From the moment of her birth the Panaghia was a miraculous answer to the prayers of Joachim and Anna and she lived "in unbroken and conscious communion with God. The whole of her life was an uninterrupted transcendence of the tendency towards evil, and a continuous ascent and progress toward virtue. With her holy Life, Our Lady surpassed the stage of asceticism and purification."[77] According to tradition she was raised in the Temple for much of her younger life, already becoming aware of a world greater than this one, preparing through stillness and prayer for the immense struggle she would undertake beginning with the greeting of the Archangel Gabriel. "Hail Mary full of Grace, the Lord is with thee."[78] Gabriel told her that the Holy Spirit would come upon her and she would conceive within her womb a son who would be holy, the seed of David and the Son of God. Her response to this strange noetic greeting was a recognition that it was beyond human comprehension. Even so, her response was without hesitation. "Behold, I am the handmaiden of the Lord. Let it be done to me according to Thy word."[79] Then her heart leapt with joy that found expression in an inspired hymn of thanksgiving and praise springing up like a vine from the soil of her heart's Grace-engendered humility.

At that moment, the call and response between Mary and the uncreated God was marked by the conception within her of one who

---

76 The Hebrew word יָדַע "yada" carries the connotation of this deep experiential knowing that has both fleshly and noetic dimensions as in Gen 4:1 "Adam knew (yada) his wife and she conceived and bore Cain." and in Isaiah 43:10 where the prophet writes "God's people have been chosen to know (yada) Him. The prophet (Jeremiah 24:7) declares "I will give them a heart to know (yada) me." These instances point toward the unconfused joining of the created and uncreated natures seamlessly united in the person of Christ and the heart of man.

77 Ephraim, A. "The Sinlessness of Our Most Holy Lady," *Analogia*, Athens, Greece: St. Maxim the Greek Institute, No. 1, September, 2016, p. 25.

78 Lk. 1:28.

79 Lk. 1:38.

was fully God and fully human at the same time. Consider what this would do to her. She was filled with more Grace that acted on her whole being. Her whole life became embodied prayer. Fr. Georges Florovsky calls this moment "a premature Pentecost. In other words, what happened to the Virgin at the Annunciation was a purification, according to the Fathers; not a purification from personal sins, which did not exist, but 'an addition of graces.'"[80] On a daily basis, her very flesh would be experienced in a different way because of sanctification by union with the deified Christ, and her mind would interpret everything through the noetically revealed mystery of her union with the uncreated world through her Son. She had offered to God the chalice of her heart as a womb for noetic prayer and her womb became the Ark of the New Covenant, where her human flesh and blood mingled with the uncreated divine essence of the *Logos*. Thus, the Church hymns that her "womb became more spacious than the heavens" for it contained the only eternally begotten Son of God. She became a living *anaphora*, continuously offering up her own body and blood for all humanity as the meeting place of the uncreated and created worlds of heaven and earth. Her ascetical forbearance grew daily, strengthened noetically by grace. Every ache and pain in her body, every uncertainty in her mind associated with her pregnancy,[81] and all that would come after, now became reminders that she was participating with body and soul in a co-creative action with the uncreated Creator. She carried the Lord's life within both her heart and her body and she would ascetically endure whatever was necessary to protect and serve this Life. Her *hesychia*[82] grew, strengthening her forbearance. The Apostle Luke relates that she would pray by pondering all these things in stillness and silence. She did this in the face of all sorts of misunderstandings swirling around her. If Joseph's

---

80   Cited in Ephraim, A., "The Sinlessness of our Most Holy Lady." p. 23.

81   Holy Tradition holds that the birth of Christ was supernatural, and that Mary remained a virgin before and after birth, not experiencing the pains of childbirth, because his delivery was miraculous. Beyond the ontological significance of this, the Holy Fathers did not elaborate further dogmatically on her experience of the pregnancy, which remains a mystery.

82   Greek word meaning deep stillness and silence which is preparatory to interior noetic prayer of the heart as described in the authors of the *Philokalia*.

own struggle[83] to help her avoid public disgrace is any indication, she endured the pain of scandal and whispers of people looking askance at her for becoming pregnant out of wedlock. Then after giving birth, for a time she became a refugee fleeing her homeland to escape the soldiers of Herod seeking to murder all the children two years and younger. Still, her unspoken prayer and the results of her obedience to God could be understood as fulfilling the prayer, "Lord, love the world through me."

From these mysteries of her life, we can see that prayer is not sitting on a lily pad in peaceful, undisturbed bliss, nor is it having a magic carpet to fly above all life's physical challenges. Rather it is an essential means of entering into embodied life more deeply and facing the difficult circumstances of this world by the power of faith in the invisible world beyond it. Prayer involves keeping watch deep in the heart, secretly protecting the flame of love and faith that grows there, from onlookers who would not understand. Prayer is freedom from vainglorious posing, constantly angling for human attention, and from useless distractions and trivialities. Prayer is mental, physical and emotional sobriety. The Holy Theotokos' humility is a witness to us of all these things. She did not lose her treasure by having her spiritual life paraded around for everyone to see. She kept it privately and her Father in heaven Who sees in secret rewarded her in secret[84]. Her faith grew and her understanding of the divine mystery further developed through years of intimately knowing her Son and trusting God as the tension between Jesus and the fallen world became more and more apparent.

By standing at the Cross watching her Son's murder, bearing the full human agony of a mother's grief, while trusting the unseen God who appeared to have abandoned Him, she became a sign for all time of the fullness of prayer in an embodied life lived among people

---

83 Mt. 1:19.

84 A hieromonk commenting on Matthew 6:4 "ὁ βλέπων ἐν τῷ κρυπτῷ ἀποδώσει σοι ἐν τῷ φανερῷ." writes, "*He who sees in the hidden place rewards you in a way that is clear and obvious.* It all takes place in that hidden realm of the heart, but the reward is palpable in ways that extend beyond the noetic, but to that particular person. This is something monks experience very much so and I think the principle is incarnational."

in humility, faith and love. The pain she felt as the Lord's mother, spoken of by the prophecy "and a sword shall pierce your soul,"[85] is beyond our comprehension. St. Silouan writes:

> We cannot thoroughly comprehend her grief. Her love was complete. She had an illimitable love for God and her Son but she loved the people, too, with a great love. What must she have felt when those same people whom she loved so dearly, and whose salvation she desired with all her being, crucified her beloved Son? We cannot fathom such things, since there is little love in us for God and man.[86]

In her, the words of Christ given two thousand years later to St. Silouan were already evident, "Keep your mind in hell and despair not."[87] She is the foremost icon of the mystery of the treasure of divine Grace kept inviolate in an earthen vessel whom we magnify as truly worthy of the title, "the birthgiver of God." The Holy Theotokos' destiny is bound up with her Son. She and Christ both, in different ways, translate the divine mercy into human terms. Both bear the wound of love that pierces the heart revealing at the darkest moment, a mysterious consolation known in abject humility and stillness of faith: "God's marvelous love is made known to man when he is in the midst of circumstances that cut off his hope."[88]

For us in the world living ordinary lives, we do well to follow her example and ask for her intercessions. We too must discover stillness and watchfulness in the cave of the heart and learn to attend to what is heard in silence while living ordinary lives in the world as she did. Deep interior prayer is not something only for the monastics or for a hermit far off in the desert. In fact, Clement of Alexandria, who directed the catechetical school of Christians in Alexandria, Egypt

---

85 Lk. 2:35.
86 Sophrony, A. *St. Silouan the Athonite*, p. 390.
87 cf. Sophrony, A. St. *Silouan the Athonite*. Essex, England: Stavropegic Monastery of St. John the Baptist, 1991.
88 Homily 72, *The Ascetical Homilies of St. Isaac the Syrian* revised second edition. Trans. From the Greek and Syriac, Boston, MA: Holy Transfiguration Monastery. 2011, p. 504.

in the early part of the 2nd century when many still were alive who had known the Apostle John and other direct disciples of the first Apostles who were witnesses of the Resurrection, and the extraordinary rise of the early church, wrote in his *Miscellanies,*

> True manhood is shown not in the choice of a celibate life; on the contrary the prize in the contest of men is won by him who has trained himself by the discharge of the duties of husband and father and by the supervision of a household, regardless of pleasure or pain—by him, I say, who in the midst of his solicitude for his family shows himself inseparable from the love of God and rises superior to every temptation which assails him through children and wife and servants and possessions.
>
> On the other hand, he who has no family is in most respects untried. In any case, as he takes thought only for himself, he is inferior to one who falls short of him as regards his own salvation, but who has the advantage in the conduct of life, inasmuch as he actually preserves a faint image of the True Providence.[89]

This may seem an unusual observation in that it holds up married persons rather than monastics as paradigmatic of the struggle for maturity in Christ. But we should remember that it is from the early centuries after the first Apostles, some of whom, like Peter, were married and who lived lives contending with the worldly difficulties and relationships that accompany this, along with the struggles of the first centuries of Christianity.

A well-known Serbian Elder in our time, based on his experiences as a monastic, suggests a similar perspective as Clement and points to the common thread of prayer and ascetical struggle in faith that makes the difference between married or monastic in whether we mature in Christ.

> It is easier in a monastery. Here we are free from all the shocking things of the world. There are few connections

---

89 *Miscellanies*, 12, ANF2, p. 543.

with the outside world and that is a good thing. Of
course, much depends on the person. That which is
required of monks and nuns is also required of lay people. Even the Holy Fathers say that the only difference
between monastics and lay people is that lay people are
married. It is easier for monastics, for they do not bear
the burdens of married life; they do not have to strive
to raise children to be good Christian and lead them
onto the right path. A monk strives for himself only. Of
course, he must pray for the whole world, but it is much
easier for him. But a lay person can achieve a much
higher level of spirituality in meekness and humility
than one who has lived as a monk in celibacy all his life,
yet has not striven to achieve perfection, he who does
not pray has no use for a holy place of holy things.[90]

The point is "whatever our work or activity," St. Symeon the New
Theologian explains, "it is the life led for God that is most blessed."[91]
Attempts to try and argue theoretically that the monastic way of life
or the married one is superior to the other or that being alone in the
desert or in the city is more conducive to spiritual growth and the
other is misguided. As the editors of the *Philokalia* point out, sum-
marizing St. Symeon, "The best and highest form of life is, for each
one, the particular way to which he or she is called. The fullness of
contemplation is accessible to married people living in the cities as
well as to the desert dweller."[92] Together in community, whether in
the monastery or in the world, we are members of the Lord's Body.
Whether married or celibate, whenever we "eat this bread and drink
this cup" in remembrance of Him, we ourselves are re-membered and
Christ is in our midst.

"But how can this be?" we might say, as the Theotokos did to the
greeting of the Archangel. Throughout the Divine Liturgy the deacon

---

90 Elder Thaddeus of Vitovnica, Our *Thoughts Determine Our Lives*. St. Herman of Alaska Brotherhood, 2009, p. 102.

91 *The Philokalia*, Vol. IV, p. 43.

92 Ibid., p. 14.

and priest call out repeatedly, "Let us attend!" This is a reminder to be embodied, to stand well, and to seek the place of the heart. "Let us stand in awe. Let us be attentive that we may present the Holy offering in peace."[93] The call and responses of the Divine Liturgy are not to be in disembodied words, lest we ourselves remain disembodied. If our lips move without our hearts, then we are in danger of being the people to whom the prophet Isaiah admonished: "These people draw near me with their mouths and honor me with their lips while their hearts are far from me."[94] The word of God is meant to penetrate the flesh and unite with it, leading to a union between the two so that they dwell together fulfilling the words of the prayer the Lord taught his disciples to pray. "Thy [uncreated] will be done on earth as it is [among the Holy Trinity] in heaven."[95]

All of the Divine Liturgy is a communal prayer of aloneness, together with one another. *Alone together* is more than social relationships or individual subjectivity. We are oriented toward the spiritual conception of the hidden person that occurs in the womb of the heart with the meeting of flesh and Spirit, of creation and the uncreated order by sharing Christ between us, within us and beyond us. It is a taste of things to come, a preparation for the encounter with Christ at our death which will reveal the depth and quality of our prayer and choices over a lifetime. Elder Sophrony describes the moment of this encounter:

> The whole of our life in its final actualization will appear as a kind of integral act, without any duration. In other words, it will be immediately 'visible', by anyone with appropriate insight, as a single whole. In that sense, every moment—even fleeting inner stirrings—leaves some traces upon the overall sum of our life.[96]

93 From the Divine Liturgy of St. John Chrysostom.
94 Isaiah 29:13.
95 Mt. 6:10.
96 Sophrony, A. *We Shall See Him As He Is*. Alaska: St. Herman of Alaska Brotherhood, 2006. p. 60.

This is because every thought (*logismos*) is a kind of vibration with a magnetic charge of sorts seeking to attract desire in us and amplify it with imagination. Such thoughts are capable of attracting our attention in this way if we are not guarding our hearts. If our attention hooks up with the thought even for a moment of hesitation as we "weigh" its charm against a corresponding desire within us, then it grows in force and begins to enlarge within the psyche. St. Neilos the Ascetic refers to a *logismos* as an "ant-lion"[97] which seems insubstantial like an ant in the beginning when it first appears, but if we feed it with our attention, it begins to grow by combining with our own desires and imagination into the power of a lion which begins to devour our energies and bring us into captivity. Every such thought is capable of leaving a mark on us if we do not let it pass, like email from a spammer, unopened, through the cyberspace of our minds. If a thought appears and I begin to attend to it with pleasure, it leaves a trace on my heart and a neuropeptide[98] imprint in my body. I can go to confession, but the effects of this stain remain on me with a potential to sprout up again from the ash heap, if, like Lot's wife,[99] I should look back over my shoulder in longing for what I have left behind.

The book of my life will be read at one time and my heart will break over every evil thought I have allowed to make an imprint on my body as I meet my Bridegroom. I will weep because I wanted to offer back to the Lord a response worthy of His pure self-offering love but I have failed. Yet a crushed and humble heart He will not despise.

Christ offers Himself to us and our response to this mystery cannot simply be complacency, wandering attention, imagination and the surfeit of passions. As earthen vessels, like the Holy Theotokos, we have the potential to receive into us a transforming noetic fire that reveals every hair on our head valuable. Every sparrow that falls from

---

97   Palmer, G.E.H., Sherrard, P., Ware, K. (eds.) *The Philokalia*. Ascetic Discourses, Vol. I, London: Faber & Faber, 1979, p. 233.

98   Neuropeptides are small protein-like molecules used by neurons to communicate with each other. They are neuronal signaling molecules that influence the activity of the brain and the body in specific ways.

99   Vid. Gen. 19:26.

a tree is noticed with pain of heart by the Only Lover of Humankind. How valuable God considers whom He has found valuable enough to be His dwelling place? Like the bush that Moses saw burning yet not consumed, when the human heart is illumined with that same noetic fire it seeks only to live out to the fullest extent of its meaning the prayer being born within it, "Lord, love the world through me!"

God created the world and called it very good. Then He placed humankind in the world with the potential to offer up everything in thanksgiving and receive God through every part of it. St. Gregory Palamas was quite emphatic about how when our inner world is healed of the passions and restored to its proper harmony, we are drawn beyond the visible creation toward the invisible God through our very sensory appreciation of creation. "The reason mankind was brought into being by God was so that they might apprehend with their senses the sky, the earth, and everything they contain, as visible objects, and by means of them go beyond them with their minds to invisible beauties, that they might sing the praises of God, the one creator of all.[100]

Prayer and watchfulness require a very fine quality of attention that includes a different relationship with our embodied selves in the present moment than we typically have. Our Lord has assumed our full human nature, body and soul, even as we seek to attend to the uncreated Lord who is also beyond us, by drawing the mind toward the heart within. In this sense, as Archimandrite Meletios Webber reminds us, "Prayer is going deeper into the body."[101] Humankind, like earth and sky and sea are also part of creation. And yet we are capable of seeing 'through' creation to the Creator Whose breath raises us up from the earth into breathing embodied souls. It is paradoxical, something our increasingly disembodied modern culture with its short attention span, cannot be still deeply enough or long enough to appreciate. We are hungry for the easy pleasures of acquiring new information which do not allow our minds to inhabit the collected place of contemplation which involves not just automatic

100 Veniamin, Christopher (trans.) *Saint Gregory Palamas the Homilies.* Homily 53, Pennsylvania: Mount Thabor Publishing, 2014, p. 421.
101 , p. 76.

mechanical attention, but an active relational *presence*. A change in our habits is very important when we begin to consider the Orthodox writings on prayer, for example those of the *Philokalia* and other texts from the ascetics and saints who lived very different lives than ours. Our starting place needs to be relational and intentionally embodied, rather than in the distracted psychic form of our typical workday attention, preoccupied as it usually is, with the "cares of the world" in such a way that we are drained of the energy we need to pray.

For this reason, in addition to the distraction of the passions which find greater purchase in us to the degree that we lack embodied attention, finding and living from the heart may be a difficult life-long struggle, but it is not a complicated one. The entrance to the heart is found where repentance, compunction and humility coalesce. These are a response of faith and love for Jesus Who says, "Behold I stand at the door and knock. If anyone hears my voice and opens the door, I will come in and share a meal with him and he with me."[102] As we have responded unto the least of these, and unto our spouses, friends, fellow church members, and anyone else we meet, we have done so unto Christ. We cannot live on this earth without being faced with the dilemma of what it means to live from the heart and yet culturally we have long ago departed from the norms that governed village life such as *philotimo*[103], which at one time the average Greek villager understood and practiced naturally from the depths of one's soul.

Orthodox theologian Olivier Clement observes:

> People in the west are today so uptight, tense, nervous, confined to the surface of life that they need to calm

---

102   Rev. 3:20.

103   Φιλότιμο is a Greek word referring to the humility and simple love that moves a person to give back more than one has received, not out of debt, but out of joy and a humble sense of shared humanity. "According to St. Paisius, *philotimo* is "a reverent distillation of goodness, the love shown by humble people, from which every trace of self has been filtered out. Their hearts are full of gratitude towards God and their fellow men, and out of spiritual sensitivity, they try to repay the slightest good which others do for them." *Spiritual Struggle*. Souroti, Greece: Holy Monastery of St. John the Theologian, 2010, preface.

themselves and to go more deeply into the meaning of the body and of the poetry of things before approaching traditional ascetic practices. These are designed for people of ancient cultures, cultures of silence and a slow pace.[104]

Our starting point for prayer must include an intentional embodied presence that is grounded in an intentional receptivity to God from the earth of ourselves: "Thy will be done on earth as it is in heaven." Both soul and body play their parts. St. Gregory of Sinai explains that "the physical senses and the soul's powers have an equal and similar, not to say identical, mode of operation, especially when they are in a healthy state; for then the soul's powers live and act through the senses, and the life-giving Spirit sustains them both."[105] This unity of mind and body helps counteract the compulsive disembodied hunger for more information that satiates the mind with knowledge without real understanding that can be lived. Elder Sophrony in one of his letters to David Balfour describes the intensity of his collected mind-body presence in prayer such that "all my being is drawn together—that is, both soul and body; that is, mind, heart, all the members of my body and even my bones."[106]

Knowledge is only a reflection of what is true, a passing mental presence that enables a glimpse of the territory but without enabling the transformation that occurs when 'standing under' the truth of it bodily with ascetical fidelity and internally gaining the discernment that arises only with the experience of authentic noetic encounter. Knowing about God is not the same as undergoing the transformation without end that occurs through communion with Him.

Another important aspect of prayer is that it is a form of *presence* and relational intimacy that resists being willfully forced based on some agenda that we have. In other words, we shouldn't approach relationship with God by a prearranged expectation that we try to

---

104   Clement, Olivier, "Life in the Body" *The Ecumenical Review.* World Council of Churches. p. 137.

105   Palmer, Sherrard and Ware, eds., *Philokalia,* Vol. IV, p. 233.

106   *Striving For The Knowledge of God, Letters to David Balfour,* Essex, England: Stavropegic Monastery of St. John the Baptist, 2016, p. 273.

make it happen willfully or try to choreograph it with our imagination or emotionality. We need to learn to be simple and open to God in love. Martin Laird makes a valuable observation of what makes for intimacy with God when he says, "You enter the land of silence by the silence of surrender, and there is no map of the silence that is surrender."[107] In other words, we can't make ourselves "do" silence. The very efforts of "doing something" disturb the silence, and yet, unless we are repeatedly defeated in our efforts to be still, we do not discover the paradoxical stillness that is embodied and attentive to the uncreated, active and yet effortless.

Once when a well-known American philosopher of religion was visiting Metropolitan Anthony Bloom's church in England, he asked him about a certain absence of emotion in his voice that he noticed during his sermons. He made a similar observation in regard to the chanting of the choir in the Russian Orthodox Church in London where Met. Anthony served. Met. Anthony responded, "Yes, that is quite true. It has taken years for that, but they are finally beginning to understand … Emotion must be destroyed. We have to get rid of emotions … in order to reach …feeling."[108] For one to be moved by the chanting, the Divine Liturgy and the whole sequence of holy days that make up the full experience of the Church, in a way that is deeper than mere emotional enthusiasm and beyond what the rational intellect on its own can encompass, a deeper encounter between mind and body is required. Met. Anthony continued, "For this to occur you have to be in a state of prayer, otherwise it passes you by… In the state of prayer one is *vulnerable*."[109] It is the same for the iconographer who learns to render the sacred mages while in a state of prayer. Chanters learn to allow chanting to emerge through them in prayer without distortion by human egotism and display. Prayer is born to the degree that we are released from vainglorious striving so that our bodies and minds are allowed to naturally be responsive to the truth. It may take years before I begin to discover

107   Laird, Martin. *Into the Silent Land: A Guide to the Christian Practice of Contemplation.* Oxford University Press: England. 2006. p. 3.

108   Needleman, J. *Lost Christianity.* New York: Doubleday & Company, p. 24.

109   Ibid., p. 25.

the difference between praying by trying to put my best side forward like the Pharisee in the Gospels,[110] showing God my portfolio, versus coming before Christ as I am without anything but awareness of my own sin and hope in God's mercy. Gradually I begin to learn that what I am trying to do and make happen in prayer is not the Way. Love is never a self-directed monologue. I need the Holy Spirit's help. If I have begun to learn this one thing alone after forty years, it is worth the price.

Real stillness is a presence arising from humility that is born of repentance in dialogue. The mind is actively drawn within the body in such a way that it becomes possible to be aware from the heart of any tensions or emotional attachments and imagination that masquerade as God. St. Mark the Ascetic says that three giants stand in the way of prayer: ignorance, forgetfulness, and laziness.[111] All of these have to do with lack of collected attention and with an inability to truly be sober and still because of weak repentance. Often such a state is characterized by a lot of busyness and unnecessary movements of body, soul and imagination. St. Mark says, "the intellect cannot be still unless the body is still."[112] St. Macarius of Egypt is equally emphatic: "Understanding cannot enter you unless you practice stillness."[113]

So, we prepare ourselves to pray by freeing our bodies from unnecessary movements and our attention from mechanically wandering about. There is a gentle intentionality and alertness to the stillness of an embodied presence that must be renewed again and again as we notice that we have unknowingly slipped under the spell of the three giants of inattention once again. St. Mark the Ascetic points out that prayer requires unity between mind and body. "When our mind and flesh are not in union, our state deteriorates."[114] This subtle

---

110   Vid. Lk. 18:11–12.

111   Vid. *The Philokalia*, Vol. I, p. 159.

112   Palmer, G.E.H., Sherrard, P. and Ware, K. *Philokalia Vol I* London: Faber & Faber, 1979, p. 128.

113   From The first Syriac Epistle, Appendix B, *The Ascetical Homilies of Saint Isaac the Syrian*, Holy Transfiguration Monastery, Boston, Massachusetts 2011, p. 160.

114   Palmer, G.E.H., Sherrard, P. and Ware, K. *Philokalia Vol I* London: Faber

inner activity of cultivating presence is true not only for prayer but for life in general. When I am inattentive and lack watchfulness, I grow dull and lack gratefulness and respect for the world and the people around me. I discover that true aliveness involves the call and response of prayer continuously. I begin to re-member that I *am present now* because I am re-membered by Christ Who is actively seeking to love the world through me. St. John Climacus describes the hesychast's intentional remembering as striving "to confine his incorporeal being within his bodily house, paradoxical as this is."[115] It is the same for us in the world. We are invited to *show up* to a call that is issued from beyond creation itself. We are creation's royal priesthood who are called to lift up creation in thanksgiving, for blessing with each breath. This ascetical labor of heightened awareness and intention to form a unified presence for prayer is an action unique to human beings. We have a special capacity for collective attention and obedience of the body, soul, mind, and breath[116] seeking communion with Christ from the heart that is different than all other creatures. That difference is that we are motivated by conscious awareness and love for the One in Whose Image we are made and in this way, we grow toward maturity in His likeness, which is the full stature, potential and measure of a human being.

& Faber. (1979) p. 129.

   115   St. John Climacus, *The Ladder of Divine Ascent* (1959) p. 237.

   116   St. Anthony points out that there are four kinds of living beings distinguished by the relationship between body, mind, soul and breath. "Some of them are immortal and have souls, such as angels; others have mind, soul and breath, such as men; yet others have soul and breath such as animals; and others have life, such as plants." Kadloubovsky, E., Palmer, G.E.H. *Early Fathers from the Philokalia*, London: Faber & Faber, 1976, p. 38.

Chapter 4

LORD, LET ME LOVE THE WORLD THROUGH YOU

Glory to the Spiritual, Who was pleased to have a Body, that in it His virtue might be felt, and that He might by that Body show mercy on those in His household.

—St. Ephraim, Hymns on the Nativity

IT IS A LOT EASIER to imagine being a world-famous pianist playing one of the most difficult repertoires in the concert hall than to practice scales to learn how to play the piano in the first place. Prayer is the same way. It is a whole lot easier to enjoy the self-calming illusions of our imagination that we are praying than to actually be attentive and pray. Met. Anthony Bloom compared prayer to "entering a lion's den."[117] Most of us wouldn't do very well when faced with a hungry lion. Waking up to our real embodied situation which unfolds between the unseen God and the uncontrollable forces of nature, human relations and "powers, principalities and spiritual wickedness in high places,"[118] is what Christians began to call the "arena." It is where we are sifted by temptations and brought to the threshold of prayer through struggles and repentance.

Like Jacob at the Jabbok River[119] and Job in the whirlwind[120], our sins are revealed by love of Christ in ways that break our hearts and remake them, little by little over a lifetime. As in Marjorie William's beloved children's story, The Velveteen Rabbit, it is when our hair is rubbed off, an eye is missing and we are decorated with various scars and failures that we are on the verge of becoming real. Prayer is a response to being loved. Repentance deepens as other people and

---

117 Anthony Bloom. *Beginning to Pray*. New York: Paulist Press, 1970.
118 Eph. 6:12.
119 Vid. Gen. 32:22–32.
120 Vid. Job 38:1.

creation begin to matter to us and the arrogance and complacency of our confidence in our own human powers are humbled with the self-confrontations occurring with adversity and age.

One of my colleagues, Dr. George Zubowicz, beloved psychiatrist and medical director of the psychiatric hospital that was part of the Institute where I work, was a Russian bear of a man who had never suffered physical illness. He was winning senior Olympic swim meets in Europe in his 80's. Inevitably, he was the one whom staff always turned to go after AWOL patients who left the hospital without permission. In a few minutes, he would return, with the person following him as docile as a lamb.

George's physical vitality and strength of will were such that when he was training for the Olympics as a young man, pushing himself to the limits of physical endurance, he told me that at one point he heard an inner voice inside him that audibly spoke to him and said, "You can continue, but you will die." He had discovered that his mind could choose to push his body to a place that it would respond to his will even at the cost of his own life and he stopped.[121]

In the last months of his life as he was dying of cancer, I used to visit him. He was so weak he could barely get out of bed to use the bathroom. One day after listening to him dispassionately describe observations of himself I said, "It seems from what you are saying that you cannot comprehend how inwardly in your 'I', your mind, you feel as strong as you ever have, yet outwardly your body is now too weak to respond to your will." He said in his thick Russian accent, "You understand me exactly."

Then he gave me a gift I will never forget. He continued, "Can you imagine, for fifty years I have been a psychiatrist. In the hospital and the nursing homes, I go from one room to the next, and I ask how the patient is and I write down his answer in my notes. Only

---

121   St. Anthony describes a hierarchy of powers. "In the body is the soul, in soul is mind, and in mind is word." *Early Fathers From the Philokalia.* p. 31. In the sanctified person, it is the *Logos* which commands and instructs the mind (spirit) which governs the soul (desires) which animates the body. Whereas, "souls not bridled by reason and governed by the mind which restrains, steadies and directs (correctly) their passions—i.e. pleasure and pain—perish like dumb beasts, for their reason is swept along by passions, like a driver by a runaway horse." p. 32.

now do I realize that in all those years, I have not known how to ask, 'How are you?' because I have never known weakness." I could only admire his struggle for objective scientific precision up to his last breath, as he dispassionately observed his own life, the way he had so many others. The compassion, simplicity, and humility revealed in his last days as he shared his discoveries with me, was heart-rending and precious.

It is by wrestling all night with an adversary he could not overcome that Jacob received the blessing of a holy wound and his new name, "Israel" which means "one who struggles with God."[122] The Holy Theotokos received a sword in her heart along with her Son. Peter and each of the Apostles who initially abandoned Jesus, running away from the Cross, later in their lives all died violent deaths as martyrs. John alone, who did not run from the Cross, died a natural death, having the daily events of his life, exile and ministry unto old age as his martyrdom.

We often hear that the name Bethlehem means "House of Bread" but there is a deeper meaning. The word *"Beth"* in Hebrew means house, but the word *"Lehem"* has two meanings. The first refers to leavening dough in order to make bread. The second means "hand-to-hand combat." Like dough we are stretched and wounded in the process of contending with God and one another as we are invisibly leavened by Grace and heated up by the fires that arise in facing the limits of our capacities. The word Bethlehem might be more

---

122   In Gen. 32:28 it is written of Jacob. "Your name shall be Israel (from the Hebrew yisra'el) which is translated "he that struggles with God. This appears to be made up of *sara* ("he fought or contended") and *el* (God). Cf. http://www.etymon-line.com/index.php?term=Israel. The Septuagint translation reads: "Israel shall be thy name; for thou hast prevailed with God, and shalt be mighty with men." The name Israel has also been interpreted by various Holy Fathers allegorically as meaning "one who beholds God." An early attribution of the meaning "one who sees God" may go back to Philo of Alexandria and Clement from whom Evagrius Ponticus picked it up and passed it on. For example, St. Macarios the Egyptian in Homily 47:5 wrote: "For *Israel* is interpreted as being the mind contemplating God." (*Pseudo-Macarius: The Fifty Spiritual Homilies and the Great Letter,* George A. Maloney, ed., New York: Paulist Press. 1992, p. 234.) These two definitions reflect the existential and ontological dimensions of the ascetical struggle on earth to be obedient to the will of God in heaven, which is born out of the noetic encounter with God.

accurately rendered "house of struggle." Jesus, the Savior of Israel (*those who struggle with God*), is born in the *house of struggle* with Man. By receiving into our bodies and souls, the Body and Blood of Him who *is* this struggle of the created and uncreated natures seamlessly wed in one person, we are being drawn into His life which is the arena where we face the lions of that same struggle in the world until the end of time. What He told his disciples remains true for all. "If they persecuted Me, they will persecute you also."[123] The Cross is the tree of life planted right in the middle of the struggle of human existence. When we say "Christ is in our midst" we are acknowledging that He meets us in the midst of the struggle which grows more intense as we pray with our lives, "Lord, let me love the world through You" all the way to hell if necessary.

It is vital to keep in mind that our contention is not with bodily processes in and of themselves, but with something much deeper, more inward and much more tenacious. It is sin originating from the deep heart[124] that disturbs and disharmonizes the processes of soul and body. "According to St. Gregory Palamas, the struggle of asceticism is not to be understood in opposition to the body or to human nature itself, but rather as the liberation of the body and human nature from sin which has made the natural functions of the human soul unnatural. Since man is both soul and body and since his body expresses his personal hypostasis (essence), he also gains the Kingdom of God *with* and *in* his body as well."[125] St. Hesychius points out that purification proceeds from inside out. "An intellect that does not neglect its inner struggle will find that ... the five bodily senses, too, are freed from all external evil influences"... and gradually, "withdraws the senses almost completely into itself."[126] By exercising ascetical fidelity toward the well-being of our soul so that

---

123   Vid. Jn. 15:18–25.

124   Mt. 15:19–20. "Jesus said, "Out of the heart come evil thoughts, murders, adulteries, fornications, thefts, false witnesses, blasphemies. These things are what defile a man.""

125   Keselopoulos, A. (2004) *Passions and Virtues According to Saint Gregory Palamas.* St. Tikhon's Seminary Press: South Canaan, Pennsylvania, p. 209.

126   St. Hesychius the Priest 53, On Watchfulness and Holiness, *Philokalia, Vol. I,* pp. 171–172.

our bodily powers are not disharmonized, while rendering ourselves available to be gradually transformed noetically by Grace acting invisibly through the attentiveness of our minds drawn to our hearts in repentance, the effects of the divine energies are transmitted to body and soul together. This unity is vital both for the conduct of our daily lives as well as in preparation for our deaths. For as St. Anthony explains, "as body without soul is dead, so soul without mind is inactive (barren) and cannot inherit God."[127] The relationship between soul and mind is formed over a lifetime by the nature of their interaction while in the body. St. Anthony makes an important and instructive observation. "Just as you treat the soul while it is in the body, so it will treat you on leaving the body."[128]

With the first gift of divine Grace we are wounded by Christ's undying love for the world. In modern terms, we could say that in the person of Christ, God willingly suffers a human trauma[129] resulting from allowing humanity freedom to sin against Him. He willingly undergoes the suffering, humiliation and death of the cross in order to offer us divine life without compelling us. The path to fully embracing the divine life also proves traumatic to humanity[130] because of the uncertainties that are part of sin which involves the

---

127 *Early Fathers from the Philokalia.* p. 35.

128 Ibid., p. 34.

129 I am not suggesting that Christ developed Post Traumatic Stress Disorder, but that He chooses to be truly affected by the suffering of humanity in order to leave humanity able to freely respond to Him without coercion. Gospel accounts as well as confirming forensic studies of the Holy Shroud reveal evidence of extensive physical trauma to the body. Gospel testimony reveals that by consciously and willingly enduring the cross, Christ protected and saved humanity. There is a paradox here. By willingly allowing himself to be helpless in the face of evil unleashed against Him, He conquers death by dying. It is known that the strongest prophylactic against developing PTSD after trauma, is being able to do some small thing to help someone, rather than merely be victimized. In suffering and dying Christ does precisely this. His action saves humanity and opens the door for us to enter on a path that loves and forgives others as He does.

130 Humanity comes to know the heart of Christ by sharing the Cross, and as Christians, willingly bearing the suffering inflicted by others, confessing our sins, forgiving and in love, praying with pain, for the life of all persons. In this way, traumas inflicted upon humanity, whether as martyrs by blood, or martyrs through enduring the ascetical suffering of love, are willingly entered into for the joy that passes worldly understanding.

freedom of others to reject God. The effects of this suffering, throughout all of time, all falls upon Christ,[131] and to the extent that we are in
Him, it also falls upon us and waits for our response. This willingness
to undergo suffering in order to leave humanity free is at the core of
the Lord's "passion-bearing" and we share in this to the extent that
we face the difficulties and challenges of our lives with faith in the
invisible presence of Christ who sustains us while calling us beyond
the created order toward our likeness in Him. This call changes how
we face our lives. St. Peter of Damascus writes that faith is evidenced
by bearing the reality of the visible sufferings of illness, misfortunes,
loss and unjust actions of others against us, while trusting in the
invisible presence of God's Grace. This is what the Holy Theotokos
does as she looks upon her Son's execution, feeling its pathos, while
trusting in God whom Jesus calls out to at the last moment, asking
why He has abandoned Him.

Christ's love is such that in effect God says to us through the
Son, 'I am yours, do with me whatever you want.' This is the marriage proposal of the Logos waiting for our response. In our first
creation, we are immature, untested and unable to be response-able
without a lifelong struggle of repentance as we discover the limits
of our human powers and the great invitation to *become fully persons
together in Christ*. It is a struggle we would in many ways rather avoid.
Like Peter when Jesus first told him about the Cross, we want the
glory and joy of Christ without the wounds of love that His Cross
entails. This preference for the vainglory of monologue instead of
the humility and relationality of dia-Logos, is the sign of the mortal
wound we bear in our fallen natures shared with Adam and Eve. We
do not say to Christ with our whole lives and our whole hearts, "I
am yours do with me whatever you want." We do not say as did Job
ultimately did in faith, love, and humility, "Though He slays me, yet
will I trust in Him."[132]

Prayer is a slow and gradual turning undistractedly in repentance
and thanksgiving toward the Cross as the Tree of Life from which

---

131   Mt. 25:40 Jesus said, "As you have done unto the least of these you have
done unto me."

132   Job 13:15.

we receive the Eucharistic fruit, Christ the medicine of immortality. According to the beloved disciple, "The Logos became flesh and dwelled among us and we have seen his glory, the glory of the only Son of God who came from the Father, full of Grace and truth"[133] Having witnessed the Transfiguration and later the appearances of the Risen Lord in the flesh, St. John, to the end of his life, remained very concerned with the embodied human dimension of Jesus Christ, so much so that he wrote in his first letter to the churches, "This is how you can recognize the Spirit of God: every spirit that acknowledges that Jesus Christ has come in the flesh is from God."[134]

Yet this is precisely why Jesus was killed. He was viewed by his enemies as dangerous to their religion because being a man he claimed to be God. "How dare you say God can become man? This is blasphemy!"[135] Rather than honoring God, this accusation actually involves hidden pride and contempt for humanity. This is from anti-Christ, a refusal of the divine life inhabiting a mortal body. Equally off the mark, during the early years of the Church, the exact opposite understanding quickly began to prevail. Some, like Cerinthus and the Docetist movement[136] within the lifetime of the Apostles, began to view Jesus as being divine and only appearing to suffer, but not really. This was the reappearance of the same human objection that Peter succumbed to when Jesus first told him about the Cross after God had revealed to him that Jesus was the Messiah. Jesus said "Flesh and blood didn't show you that." That which is created cannot see what is uncreated without aid from above. This is ontological, not psychological, coming from outside the created order. Recognition of Christ is a noetic revelation. "No one can say Jesus is Lord except by the Holy Spirit."[137]

---

133   Jn. 1:14.

134   I Jn. 4:2.

135   Paraphrase of Mt. 26:65.

136   From the Greek δοκεῖν/δόκησις which means "to seem". The Docetists were an early Christian group who maintained that Jesus only "seemed" to suffer because his actual "human" life on earth was merely an appearance of such and not actually fully human.

137   I Cor. 12:3.

What effect do you think that had on Peter? He was suddenly raised to the head of the class above all the other apostles. Did his inner vainglorious press secretary suddenly become inflated with the opportunity for inner posturing overt his specialness? This is heady stuff. It's like he was suddenly staggering on the Jim Beam intoxication of vainglorious illusions and presumed an ability and mandate to instruct even the Lord Himself! When Jesus tells the Apostles more about what it means to be the Christ, about His suffering and the humiliation and pain of the Cross, Peter "pulled him aside and began to rebuke him."[138] Imagine that. Peter objected to the suffering of the Cross and now presumed to teach his Lord. Jesus discerned the difference that had occurred with his disciple, and his response was surely devastating as well as instructive for Peter and the others, of the clear difference between this created world and the uncreated divine life. "Get behind me Satan, for you are not on God's side, but men."[139] Wonder how Satan found his way into Peter's mind right at that moment and in only seconds after a noetic illumination? Peter went from divine revelation to beguilement in seconds. Imagine the impact on him and the others, from being recognized as the divinely inspired head of the class to being regarded as a servant of the devil. Through his humbling we can all see our own vulnerability to the same mistake. His confession recorded for us in the Gospels underscores for us the subtlety and ever present existence of temptation as well as points to the transformation of Peter the Apostle whose humility is evident in leaving us his "confession."

This proved to be a difficult and necessary intervention because the infections of pride and vainglory are very deep. According to Peter's confessions we know that even after this devastating encounter he was still insistent that he was not like other men, not like the rest of his brother disciples. He imagined and insisted that his zeal was greater than theirs. "Even if all fall away I will not."[140] St. Gregory Palamas points out[141] that Christ three times asked Peter, after

---

138 Mt. 16:22.
139 Mt. 16:23.
140 Mk. 14:29.
141 *Saint Gregory Palamas the Homilies.* (Trans.) Christopher Veniamin,

he had repented for his prophesied betrayal, "Do you love me *more than these?*"[142] meaning "more than these disciples of mine," reminding him of his earlier boasting. St. Gregory points out that this time Peter says in response only "Lord, Thou knowest that I love Thee." Only then, having acquired humility through the crushing of his heart, can the Lord ordain Peter to "feed my lambs."

Why is this so important? Satan is the spirit of anti-Christ who out of pride and vainglory has contempt for the imperfect creation and is not willing to suffer in the least for humankind. It is this anti-human impulse that constantly attracts our attention in the form of seeking perfection by way of gaining power over others along with securing the comforts, privilege and honors that go with a sense of entitlement and superiority, however disguised beneath pious lambskin. These are the ambitions of the heart of stone, the preoccupations of egotism. The Jewish philosopher Martin Buber pointed to the essence of the problem of evil when he wrote, "He who is living the life of monologue is never aware of the other as something that is absolutely not himself and at the same time something with which he nevertheless communicates…Love without real outgoing to the other, reaching to the other, and companying with the other, the love remaining with itself—this is called Lucifer."[143] Hell, then, can be understood in its essence as a refusal of *dia-Logos*, "the denial of the Eucharist, the tragic freedom of absolute narcissism, that is, the supreme self-torture of a freely chosen enmity against love."[144] The vainglorious monologue of self-love accompanies all sin and addiction which are rooted in an unyielding pride of self-sufficiency. The journey from *kenodoxia* (empty glory) to *orthodoxia* (true glory)[145] is the movement out of the poverty of our fallen

---

Pennsylvania: Mount Thabor Publishing. 2014. p. 223.

142 Jn. 21:15.

143 Buber, M. *Between Man and Man,* New York: Routledge and Kegan Paul, 1993, pp. 23–24.

144 Loudovikos, N, *Hell and Heaven, Nature and Person. Chr. Yannaras, D. Stăniloae and Maximus the Confessor Holiness: The Sacrament of Surprise, International Journal of Orthodox Theology* 5:1 (2014) urn:nbn:de:0276-2014-1027, p. 32.

145 *Kenodoxia* is an ancient Greek Patristic word referring to "empty" self-referring glory. *Orthodoxia*, according to Lampe's *Patristic Lexicon*, is generally translated

imaginary self-centered lives into the shared commonwealth of the church [cosmos] where each of us has a unique and beloved place along with all the rest.

It is said that the martyrs of the Church "give blood to receive spirit." Once, on a visit to Mount Athos, we had stopped at Philotheou Monastery. My friend Dimitri, who had been there many times over the years and knew a number of the monks, had shared with me that he was sick with cancer that ended his life soon after our trip but he had not wanted anyone else to know this at that time. We had been planning our trip to Mt Athos for a while and Dimitri learned of his diagnosis just before we were to leave. So, he had at that time a secret inner ascetical struggle while he outwardly gave no sign of it but offered his joy, friendship and generosity to everyone he met.

The day we were there, former Abbot, Elder Ephraim, had told the guest master, Fr. Giorgios, to take good care of him because he loves him a lot. Fr. Giorgios took us out into the woods on a rollicking hike, stumbling over rocks and little ravines to a small waterfall in the forest. We were stepping into holes and navigating small ledges that got more precipitous as dusk settled in. Dimitri, a physician who was always professionally attired, was in his street shoes, coat and tie and slipping all over the place. Though tired that evening, Fr. Giorgios kept us all up late into the night feeding us watermelon and fruits and speaking to us in Greek about all sorts of theological things and the need for repentance and prayer. Dimitri was translating what he said into English for me because Fr. Giorgios spoke only Greek and I was the only non-Greek-speaking person present. I kept telling Fr.

---

by the Holy Fathers as "right opinion or belief". But according to Kittel, G. (ed.) *Theological Dictionary of the New Testament, Vol II, p. 242.* "In biblical and biblically influenced Greek as a whole we hardly ever find δόξα used for opinion." Typically δόξα is used in the LXX to translate Hebrew words meaning "power," "splendor," "glory or honor." "Its primary meaning does not emerge except for reference to God." (p. 244). It is therefore in this way that I use these two Greek terms to contrast the two extremes of "empty" glory of fallen men and the "correct" or "right" glory given to God by those in right relationship with Him. This of course, would include by extension, the meaning of "right belief" or opinion' so I do not believe there is any contradiction in this.

Giorgios that Dimitri was tired and we should stop, but Fr. Giorgios kept going. I began to wonder if in some way he had discerned that Dimitri was suffering and was prophetically asking of him a greater ascetical effort in order for him to receive an even greater benefit for his unselfish labors.

The next day as we were leaving, Fr. Giorgios came up to the back window of the car where I was sitting and leaned down with his head at window level looking in and said to me in a loud voice, speaking in English for the first time since we had been together, "Stephanos, remember, He is fully God and fully Man!" I was surprised and perplexed at the time, since this was something I did not recall us discussing directly the previous day and because he spoke in English and specifically and loudly to me. He said it with such emphasis and directness that I have never forgotten it. Over the years it has proven to be something of a prophetic word, which has been central to my work as a pastoral psychotherapist and deacon, moving between the altar of the Divine Liturgy and the altar of the human heart. God did not create the entire cosmos and the diversity of creation in order to then say to us, "I don't want you to have anything to do with it." The whole point is for the creation to become holy through the God-Man Christ, with humankind serving as a royal priesthood through whom the entire creation is continually lifted up in thanksgiving and received back in blessing. Sin is a consequence, both of our freedom to become fully alive as persons, an indication of our spiritual immaturity.

Often it is cancer or some other illness or tragedy that provides the conditions of struggle in the heart that matures us and prepares us for the meeting with Christ that we have in death, the most important meeting of our lives. I saw cancer have this effect in Dimitri's life. He found precious tears he had yearned for over many years, drawing them from a wellspring of gratefulness. He called everyone he knew and with joy and humility asked for forgiveness. I wept after that conversation which was a great gift to me offering a gentle light warming the heart. Humility and love given through this generous, humbled man rendered everything precious and brought me to my heart in repentance and thanksgiving.

In both Dimitri and George's cases, two proud, incredibly pow-
erful, brilliant, accomplished, loving, generous men, found so much
Grace and humbling through the Cross of their cancer at the end of
their lives that it is possible to say "Glory to God for your mercy." I
have seen this transformation in others as well. Trauma, heartbreak
and tribulation, as St. Peter of Damascus writes, are often signs that
Grace is very near to us, a perspective echoed by Elder Ephraim who
once said, "If everything goes right for a person, I begin to fear God
has abandoned him." Grace hidden behind tragedy, is made visible in
the soul's response to the body's helplessness, failure and even more
powerfully, where there is an inner sense in the soul of being abandoned by God. In these ways, we are being invited through faith into
an interior spiritual struggle with the old addicted man of the passions so that the new hidden person of the heart who is called into
life by Grace through loving, can be born. Such struggles become our
Jabbok River rebirth.

Fully God and fully human. Heaven and earth meet in the person
of Jesus Christ and *His Cross is the presence of God in humanity's experience of God's absence.* St. Gregory of Nazianzus in the early years of
the church said of Christ's incarnation, "Whatever is not assumed
cannot be healed." Whatever God does not experience to the same
degree of loss and helplessness as we do, cannot be redeemed. If God
does not have a heart of flesh, how can we trust Him? Jesus is God's
willingness to know heartbreak for love of His creation. Elder Sophrony writes,

> In this world, Christ inevitably suffers. Were it not
> for that, we Christians could not have the boldness
> in prayer that we need. If, contrariwise, I live in ease,
> with the gratifications of the flesh, like other people do,
> authentic strength of soul, and the capacity to draw near
> to God, will not manifest themselves in me. It is not
> a matter of 'cultivating ' suffering. No—that is utterly
> inappropriate and ludicrous. It is a matter of knowing
> that through suffering we become aware of our spiritual
> freedom, aware of what separates us from the world of

animals, which are moved not by the mind, but by natural desires and instincts.[146]

One of my patients was raped physically, mentally and emotionally by her stepfather on a weekly basis from age 11 to 19. She was his secret lover in the family right under her mother and brother's nose. He told her he would be the greatest lover she ever had and would prevent her from being spoiled by boys. Because what he did to her was physically tender and all-consuming, the betrayal and injury to her heart and personality went very deep. I am her sixth therapist and we have been working together for many years as she tries to recover from the damage this did to her in so many ways. Some years into her therapy, she went to see the film, the Passion of Christ, and she told me afterward, "I cried. It was horrible what they did to Him. But you know, what happened to Him isn't as bad as what happened to me."

I said to her, "You are right. If all that happened to Jesus was that He got whipped and beaten and died a relatively short death on the Cross in a few hours, there are many, many in the world, in the Gulags and concentration camps, and secretly in homes and families like you, who have suffered worse. But what we must understand is that Christ undergoes the full conditions of human suffering from the beginning of time to the end. When you were being raped, He was too.[147] What happened to you happened to Him." This is the theology of St. Gregory Nazianzus and the Orthodox Church and it stopped her in tracks. She said "I have never considered that possibility." All she had known was the imagined far away Father-God she felt condemned by as an adulteress when she went to church. Now here was God humble and loving her enough to be fully involved in her life to the point that He was willing to undergo the full impact of all her suffering and helplessness as well as suffering the invasion and injustices it represented. In her humility, her greatest fear became "I

---

146 *Letters to His Family*, Essex, England: Stavropegic Monastery of St. John the Baptist, 2015, pp 103–104.

147 Cf. Col. 1:24; Mt. 25:40; Acts 9:5 which points to how Christ receives the blows given to those He loves.

hate for Him to have to have seen this." This realization opened a
door for her through which the Jesus Prayer began to take root in
her heart sprouting from a hope that passes human understanding.
Christ was now recognized in the secret place at the very heart of her
suffering; the place she felt most defiled and full of rage. The place of
endless sadness and hopelessness was transformed into a place from
which she might find the possibility of a different kind of love than
she had ever known. She did not ask for or deserve the hell that she
faced as an adolescent, any more than Jesus deserved crucifixion. She
had received a wound from the evil one through the stepfather she
needed and loved. Why? Because he was free to disobey God and
the wounds with which He was wounded fell on Him through her.
Contending in faith with this wound is proving to be the primary
battle ground for the formation in Christ of her deep spiritual heart.
Like Jacob, all these years, she has refused to let go of the struggle
against which she is unable to prevail psychologically, in the hope of
receiving a blessing from the wound which will carry with it a new
identity created by God who conquers death by dying and cleanses
all sin and suffering by His great mercy.

Think of that. Can you imagine the courage, humility and tenac-
ity of the divine life inspiring a soul to return for thirty years to
the call and response with another human being, trying to come to
terms like Job with the years of hell that were unleashed in her life
through no fault of her own? This is not only her ascetical labor but
has become mine to bear vicariously as well, to sit with and try not
do what the disciples did outside Gethsemane and go to sleep, to dis-
sociate from the intensity of it all. Jesus said, "Will you keep awake
and watch with Me?" He asked them. This was not just for those
there with him in Gethsemane that day, but for everyone who would
come after them. For if we run away from the suffering of the Cross
or pretend that we have a method that will overcome needing to take
up the Cross and suffer for it, then we will serve the evil one and
like Peter deserve the Lord's rebuke "Get behind me Satan, for you
are on the side of men and not God."[148] Jesus was, in effect, telling

---

148 Mt. 16:23.

them, 'I need you to be willing to be broken and consciously accept the Cross in your life and in the life of others, so you can be a human being with and for others and I can transform their lives into Mine.' Glory to Thee O Lord!

If the uncreated, invisible, immaterial God did not take on flesh, but only appeared to, as the Docetists of the first century proclaimed; if God only pretends to suffer, but doesn't really, or if Jesus was only human as the Arians and the chorus of modern theological revisionists claim, then we cannot be saved from our predicament. There is no hope. If Christ does not undergo the full human embodied situation of helplessness and injustice resulting from human freedom to disobey and reject God, then how would anyone who has undergone such defilement ever trust God? If human suffering and degradation surpass the willingness of God to undergo the same trials as creation is subjected too, what hope is there? Why would anyone have interest in such a removed, above-it-all god? The Church declares that Jesus Christ's fully uncreated divine nature and fully created human nature, are seamlessly united without loss of distinction of either nature, *in one person*. Our image, like His, bears a wound that is a sign of God's willingness to love to the point of sacrificing His own life and going to hell for the sake of His beloved. It is traumatic to Christ to create humankind and offer us the gift of uncreated divine life in so far as it entails his crucifixion. The process of receiving divine Grace over a lifetime, bearing the Cross, and being refashioned into His likeness as persons, proves to be a struggle which is beyond created human powers, as it was for Jacob who wrestled with God.

The bodily life we fear losing and the desires of our soul that we seek to offer Christ in return for His life tremble before the mind's awareness of the prospect of total annihilation and our inability to bridge the abyss between us and uncreated God on our own. A revered and memorable saying among the Athonite monks offers a different perspective. "Die before you die, so that when you die you don't have to die." Jesus said, "Unless a grain of wheat falls into the earth and dies it remains alone, but if it dies it bears much fruit."[149] One of

---

149 Jn. 12:24.

Elder Sophrony's disciples, Archimandrite Zacharias, describes the ascetical prayer vigil at the threshold of death as a

> powerful experience which is able to detach man from every attachment of this life and to disclose to him his uselessness and nothingness. Suddenly, man awakes out of his age-old stupor. He perceives that God's eternity summons him from every side, but he is as yet unable to face it directly, and there is no place in him suitable to receive it. He is cut off far from the living eternity of God, and yet, his spirit demands eternal life and nothing less can give him rest. He suffers deeply, and through this very suffering, the most significant marvel in human life begins. According to Elder Sophrony, this preliminary experience, "is the first step towards the awakening in man of the hypostatic principle."[150]

St. John wrote, "No one has ever seen God at any time; the only begotten Son, who is in the bosom of the Father, He has made Him known."[151] The single most important question of the Gospels asked again and again, upon which everything else depends, is "Who is Jesus Christ?" It is a testimony in itself that no one in the Gospels could comprehend His full nature through the five senses, by reasoning, or by any other human means. The Apostles could see and touch Jesus, and hear His teaching for three years, but they could not recognize His divinity except as it was revealed to them by God as in the case of Peter, James, and John who by divine illumination, momentarily acquired the ability to see Him as He is, a burning bush, transfigured in uncreated light on Mt Tabor. Even Mary Magdalene did not recognize the bodily Risen Jesus immediately after His Resurrection, until He called her personally by name and her spiritual eyes were opened by the personal invitation of His voice.

This is perhaps the most overlooked and unappreciated aspect of the Gospels–the invisibility of the Son of God before all who

---

150   Archimandrite Zacharias, *Man the Target of God*. Essex, England: Stavropegic Monastery of St. John the Baptist. 2015, p. 131.

151   Jn. 1:18.

presume to see and to know Him based merely on human comprehension, unaided by uncreated divine Grace. In the Gospels, those who encounter Him and receive life are blind, deaf, paralyzed, possessed, people who do not presume to know anything about Him other than daring to cry out for God's mercy, drawn to Him by their suffering and hope. By stark contrast, those who presumed to know and judge Him according to human means are shown to be blind and ignorant without realizing it. When Jesus asks His disciples, "Who do people say I am?" and Peter replies, "You are the Messiah, the Son of the Living God."[152] Jesus tells him, "Flesh and blood did not reveal this to you, but my Father who is in heaven."[153] This is confirmation of a noetic encounter, but as we learn from Peter's confession, one such revelation was not yet enough to change his worldly understanding which did not yet include knowledge of the Cross, the resurrection and the indwelling of the Holy Spirit. When Jesus began to repeatedly tell the Apostles that the Cross of love means going to hell for the sake of the beloved, this mystery remained as invisible to them as His divinity.

The heart is the tabernacle where the soul encounters the Holy Spirit. Jesus said, "Where your treasure is, there will your heart be also."[154] The greatest potential of every human being is to fulfill our calling to be the royal priesthood who become the meeting place of the created and uncreated worlds, lifting up the gifts of creation each moment from the altar of the heart, as the priest does in the anaphora of the Divine Liturgy: "Thine own of Thine own, we offer Thee, in all and for all." The Lord said, "As often as you eat and drink together, do this in remembrance of Me." In other words, as often as we live and breathe, let us do all things remembering that Christ is the Living One in whom and through Whom all creation is received and transfigured. Then we can say in thanksgiving for the unspeakable, totally undeserved gift of life, at every moment, "Christ our

---

152 Mt. 16:16.
153 Mt. 16:17.
154 Mt. 6:21.

God you are the true yearning and everlasting joy of all who love You and all creation praises You forever."[155]

---

155   From the Anonymous Thanksgiving Prayer following communion.

Chapter 5

LORD, LET ME BE LOVED BY YOU THROUGH THE WORLD

It is only with the heart that one can see rightly; what is essential is invisible to the eye.[156]

—Antoine de Saint-Exupéry

THE WORLD AS EUCHARISTIC GIFT is received when it is offered first to Christ and it is Christ Whom we seek to receive through it. God created the world and declared it "very good."[157] Every aspect of creation is an expression of God whose uniqueness testifies to the Divine presence. St. Maximos the Confessor writes,

> God is the producer and generator of tenderness and eros. He has set outside Himself what was within Himself, namely creatures. Which is why it is said of Him: God is love.[158]

Every creature, every part of creation, is created through the Logos Who expresses the Divine love and joy. But without purification of our hearts and uniting of our human powers informed by Grace, we are blind to these revelations which St. Maximus called the *logoi*, the spiritual essences of creatures that express the divine joy in unique ways. The immense diversity of embodied forms and the uncreated Creator offers a continual symphony of call and response in the heart of humanity, which is lifted up, "Thine own of Thine own we offer Thee in all and for all" in an eternal *anaphora* standing at the altar of the heart. This is our real life, the priesthood of every human being.

---

156   *Prince,* Antoine de Saint-Exupéry, *The Little Prince,* New York: Harcourt, chapter 21.

157   Gen. 1:31.

158   On the Divine Names Book IV, 4. PG 4:265C.

So why are we so often plagued by the three giants of ignorance, forgetfulness, and laziness, as St. Mark the Ascetic says?[159] Why is it that, blind to the Eucharistic nature of the world, we objectify and depersonalize it failing to see Christ in and through all things and all persons? We are blind to the extent that we do not provide sanctuary for the treasure of the Lord's presence in our hearts as sacred vessels. Like Esau, home from the hunt, we settle for the pleasure of satisfying our bodily appetites without realizing there is so much more possible if we receive everything as a revelation of God. Instead I say the words of a prayer, but then eat mindlessly like a dog.

In 1985, when I was living in Pennsylvania, I drove four and a half hours to go to confession with an Athonite Elder who was visiting a parish in Pittsburgh. I had begun seeing him whenever I could, even though I was at the time a Presbyterian pastor. On this occasion, I left confession with tears running from my eyes and a heart so full of joy and gratefulness that this continued for a half hour on my drive back home. I remember how I was observing this weeping while driving in and out of tractor trailer trucks without the slightest disturbance. When I got home, I will never forget the dinner I had with my wife and children. It was as if I had never tasted green peas and potatoes before. A joyful gratefulness for everything around me remained. Gentle, welcoming laughter bubbled up in me in appreciation of the children's presence. I noticed its quality was different than normal. There was not the slightest trace of sarcasm or frivolity at another's expense. There was a sense that everything was right with the world and my family and all was one harmonious whole; each taste, each movement, a gift deserving thanksgiving to God and accompanied by wonder. It was a taste of the way the world could be when the heart is guileless and unencumbered by passions, but it soon faded.

Many years later on a trip to Mt. Athos, a friend took us to Clochard's Restaurant in Thessaloniki, which he said was one of the finest restaurants in the world. He knew the owner and we were dazzled by dish after dish of exquisitely prepared foods which the

---

159   Vid. *The Philokalia, Vol. I*, p. 159.

chef personally brought out for us to try. I remember tasting these delicacies and appreciating each of them with my tongue as unique culinary delights, but my heart was not open in the same way as it had been so many years before. An ingredient in me was missing. During the conversation, he told us that some of the monks from Mt Athos were coming there to learn how to prepare food. That puzzled me. What are those who have "left the world" doing coming to learn how to prepare tasteful foods like a world-famous chef? When I had visited monasteries, I had noticed repeatedly that the food was always exceptionally good, but not as a result of herbs and condiments. The monks continuously pray the Jesus Prayer when they prepare the food and I had always assumed this to account for why monastic food, though simple, tastes so good. But then again, my heart was open in a different way at that time. It appeared to me that some of the monks ate quickly and seemingly without much inner embodied attention to the act of eating itself. Why would they learn to cook from a gourmet chef if they were going to ignore the unique qualities of the food and the pleasure of eating?

Some years before, arriving for the first time on Mount Athos at the Monastery of Vatopedi, after being ushered into the church to venerate the relics, which included a belt of braided camel's hair that belonged to the Holy Theotokos, we were in the Trapeza for dinner. My heart was still ringing with the silence of gratefulness and awe for the experience. I was gently alert to every sensation. Abbot Ephraim came over and handed me a tomato. "From Vatopedi," he said gently. Tears of grateful appreciation flowed again in response, as they had unexpectedly when the relic of the Holy Mother's belt had been placed in my hands. He picked up a zucchini and handed it to me smiling, "From Vatopedi." More tears. And again, an onion, saying the same thing. Each time, the impression of receiving a total unmerited gift from God washed my heart clean of everything but the essential ingredient of Grace-infused thanksgiving. I found myself in awe of the act of eating, transformed by the gift of hospitality given by the hidden labors and prayers of the monks who asked nothing in return. Later after blessed bread was passed around and I had eaten a piece, the Abbot again said, "Stephan, you like?"

The connection was beginning to be clear. I was being nourished by Grace, but only because the heart was made capable of Eucharistic humility engendered by Christ in the simplest of acts uniting body and soul in communion shared with others and through no virtue or effort of my own.

Some years later again on the Holy Mountain, I asked one of the elders about eating meals together, suggesting that the tastes of food along with appreciation for the mystery of its various transformations from mineral to plant to prayerful preparation and then its offering as a gift of hospitality through the labors and prayers of others, deserved appreciation in the form of a finer quality of attentiveness. Praying with words about eating, and then eating carnally without conscious awareness of the qualities of the food misses an important eucharistic dimension. The human gift of preparing the food, the further transformation of the food through the action of eating and digestion, all of which have been offered gratefully to God in thanksgiving for a blessing along the way, become prayer. The act of eating, like breathing, is recognized as part of a sacred action. I felt like we should intone, "Let us attend" during the eating of the meal lest we take all this for granted. Wouldn't this be far more appropriate as an extension of divine love than rushing through the meal seeking to avoid the temptation of taking pleasure in the voluptuousness of the creation, lest it prove a temptation and overcome us? Fr. Schmemann "spoke glowingly of drinking orange juice as a human act that paralleled the Eucharist. He spoke about savoring the orange juice, making the ordinary act into a sacred act. Savoring and cherishing are part of taking delight in the present moment."[160]

Surely eating can be prayer, just like growing the foods and preparing them can be? Why else would the Lord see fit to give us His life through the act of asking us to remember Him by infusing the ordinary daily action of our communal eating of bread and wine at a meal together with His own life? We take such care in all the steps of preparation for making the Prosphora and in the priestly prayers of the Liturgy. We prepare ourselves with confession and fasting and

160   Rossi, A. *Becoming a Healing Presence,* Chesterton, Indiana: Ancient Faith Publishing, 2014, p.115.

mindful attention for a personal encounter with Christ when we receive bread and wine as His holy and precious Body and Blood. Why then would we not seek to attend to the qualities of the food we eat and receive the whole experience of table fellowship and one another gratefully as gifts of God? Does the Eucharist not teach us this? When I conveyed this to the elder, he was thoughtful, smiled, and nodded his head in agreement, saying, "Monks eating rapidly without presence is not good. We are to become prayer."[161] Of course, it is easier to ask the question than to actually practice this in my life as I shamefully acknowledge.

Sometime later it happened that I was attending the first Patriarchal Health Conference in Rhodes, Greece and was sitting at the table with Abbot Dositheos, a Greek monk of some repute who had written a famous monastic cookbook. He was silent throughout most of the dinner, a reminder to me of St. Ignatius' observation that the Bishop who is silent is accorded the greatest respect! Meanwhile, I the impetuous one, was having a discussion with a hierodeacon about this issue of attention and food. I mentioned that some of the monks from Mt. Athos were traveling to Clochard's to learn how to cook and said that it seemed to me a contradiction that at the monastery the monks ate their meals quickly without attention. He snapped at me, "How would you know?!" and I responded, "I could tell by looking at the way their bodies moved when they ate." Abbot Dositheos, who had listened without saying anything until then, looked up and said to the deacon, "He is right." I don't know if that was to reprove the deacon for the scolding tone of voice he used with me, or if he really agreed with what I was saying.

The way a person moves is affected by the quality of attention that accompanies their inner life of prayer and repentance. The more Grace, the finer and subtler the changes. Each person is different, however, so the effects are somewhat different for each. Nevertheless, there are subtle cues. St. Anthony of the Desert pointed out "That a soul is truly intelligent and virtuous is shown in a man's walk, voice, smile, conversation and manner."[162] That is why someone who

---

161   Elder Antonio Gregoriatis.
162   St. Anthony. Kadloubovsky and Palmer, G.E.H. (eds.) *Early Fathers from*

went to see St. Anthony, after a long silence, when asked if he had any question, responded, "It is enough to see you, father." The presence of Grace is conveyed through change in the body's rhythms and tone. The inner disposition of the soul is revealed especially through changes in the small muscles of the face which are not directly under central nervous system control. It is possible as St. John Cassian notes, "to recognize the interior state from the look, the face, the bearing of a person."[163] St. Gregory Palamas even counseled his parishioners to notice the quality of prayerful attention through the change in a person's body in order to be near them! "When you enter the church, look for the more godly of those within, whom you can recognize just by seeing how they stand in attentive silence."[164]

> For the Fathers, the link between body and soul is so intimate that all inner attitudes must "take shape" in an external behavior. Not only do such behaviors express feelings and the dispositions of the soul, but they also allow these dispositions to truly fulfill themselves. A feeling (which is a movement of the soul) engages the depth of the human being only if it becomes incarnate in a gesture, a posture, or a bodily practice. A spiritual life that purely "internal" remains cerebral, conceptual or imaginative.[165]

Once when we were in Russia, my wife and I had the opportunity to visit Optina Monastery. We discovered that we were the first Americans who had been there in a number of years. One of the monks informed us that there were some beds in a room we could use if we needed them! The assumption was that the pampered and self-indulgent Americans would not be used to standing for the long worship service. The monastery was packed with people from wall

---

the Philokalia. London: Faber and Faber Limited. 1975, pp. 23–24.

163   Cited by Larchet, Jean-Claude, *Mental Disorders and Spiritual Healing,* New York: Sophia Perennis, 2005, p. 23.

164   *The Homilies of St. Gregory Palamas,* (Trans.) Christopher Veniamin, Pennsylvania: Mt. Thabor Publishing. 2014. p. 143.

165   Deseille, P. *Orthodox Spirituality and the Philokalia,* (A. Gythiel, trans.) Wichita, KA: Eighth Day Press, 2008. p. 119.

to wall. Outside the temperature was around 9 degrees. Many had walked for miles from surrounding villages to be there. Very few cars were in the parking lot. During the service one monk out of the 40 or 50 there caught my attention and I watched him throughout the service. His body and presence conveyed a deep quality of penitence and humility. I thought to myself, if there is one monk I would like to meet, it is that one. He is the only one out of all the rest, whose body evidenced how long repentance had opened engendered a refined attention and humility that had changed the way he was embodied down to his smallest movements and overall posture.

Later when we were eating breakfast and preparing to leave, Matushka Evgenia asked if we had gotten the blessing of Staretz Ilia. I was surprised. "I didn't know you had a staretz," I said. She told us that the Holy Theotokos had appeared to him as a child and that he was clairvoyant and people waited weeks to see him. She went and spoke to him about us and as it turned out, he was the monk I had noticed earlier. He graciously received us and spent an hour or so talking with us through an interpreter. Very clearly he had been transformed by Grace even down to the movements of his body. What happens in us when we realize someone is a Grace-bearer? We are humbled and awakened in our hearts. We hunger and thirst for something that this world cannot give and yet this gift awakens us to the world itself as a reflection of this gift. This is what happens when we approach the Holy Eucharist with "fear, faith and love." Gradually, we begin at moments to approach one another in this same way because each one is a Christ-bearer whether we recognize this or not. The giants of ignorance, forgetfulness, and laziness block our way by rendering us unaware that Christ is *fully God and fully human* without confusion and is raised bodily to the right hand of God bearing all humanity in Himself.

Our theology of icons is also a testimony to the action of Grace working through materiality because of the images that they bear. There is an icon in Taylor, Pennsylvania, at St. George Carpatho-Russian Orthodox Church that has been streaming a fragrant lemon and rose-scented myrrh over the entire surface of the icon, continuously for five years. There is so much myrrh flowing from it that the priest walks around during the services and lets the oil drip from it into the cotton balls in people's open plastic bags. This is a myrrh-gushing icon that substantially increases its flow every Pascha. Bishop Gregory of Nyssa calls it a *Tsunami* because it gushes so much fragrant oil. Why does God show us this kind of miracle if not to confirm that it is the Image in which we are made that renders creation valuable. Our bodies are mingled with this image so that we can be filled with Grace and begin to exude the virtues of Christ's own holiness. We can be salt for the earth, light-bearers who unknowingly give witness to His presence among us.

We are ensouled bodies and embodied souls. It is written in *Genesis* that God created humankind by breathing divine breath into the dust.[166] Interestingly, in the ancient Hebrew language there were no vowels. The word for God Who revealed Himself to Moses as "I AM WHO I AM" is represented by four consonants "Yod He Vaw He". Since this word was not spoken aloud except by the High priest once a year while in the Holy of Holies in the Temple on behalf of all the people, no one really knows what the name sounded like. The scribes would not even write these letters in a manuscript without washing their hands, such was the reverence of the tradition of the Holy Name. How language first developed is a great mystery. What gave rise to the first words signifying the reality of God? Breath launched a meaning from the heart that passed across the vocal chords, like a violin bow. A friend of mine who is a psychiatrist and writer in Greece, Fr. Vasileios Thermos, translated a line from one of his poems. "Every word we speak is a translation from an ancient manuscript that has been lost." Words are magic, revelations. They do not belong to us, but pass through us and we pass through them, translating the experiences of our flesh into meaning and returning to us, changing us according to their power. It is said among the Hasidic Jews, "The Spirit seeks a body through speech." As one of the oldest original languages in existence, there is speculation that the word for God's name might originally have arisen out of recognition of the sacredness and mystery of the very act of breathing itself,

---

166 Gen. 2:7.

like a whisper, a sigh, a recognition of bearing life with each breath. All living beings breathe. So it may have originally been derived from something like the in breath, (whispered) "Yaaaahhhhh... outbreath, Waaaaayyyyyy" (whispered).

Anatomically, the heart is situated between and just behind the lungs. In this way, perhaps even physically, it expresses something of the *logoi* of the relationship between the heart of flesh and the divine breath—the *ruach* or *pneuma*[167] of the divine Name that comes from beyond us bringing new life upon which we depend. Like the *manna,*[168] it comes to us unbidden and we take just what we need and no more. We cannot store it up. We learn to depend on the mercy of the Giver of Life with each breath. Breath enters into us and removes from us impurities of body and soul, cleansing and reviving us. Some of the Fathers suggest that prayer should draw breath into the heart while remembering the intention of the words, "Lord Jesus Christ Son of God..." as we breathe in and "Have mercy on me a sinner..." as we breathe out. When this rhythm is slow and one is fully embodied and very still with collected attention that is totally focused on the meaning of the prayer merged with the breathing, there is a deeper sense of what the words of Genesis may mean. Adam is drawn up into life from the dust of creation and rendered flesh (*nephesh*[169]) by the divine breath. We are *inspired.* Then we *expire.* This liturgy of call and response along with the rhythmical talanton[170] of our heartbeat embodies the awareness of our creation and our death with each breath. In this way we can never completely forget that we and everyone around us and all of creation as one harmonious whole, depend totally on God's Grace and not on ourselves, for life. Our breath and heartbeat are the sounds of the liturgy at the altar of

---

167 Hebrew and Greek words for "Spirit"

168 cf. Exodus 16:1–35.

169 In Hebrew there is no word of "individual self" as we think of in the modern era. *Nephesh* carries the meaning of embodied soul without distinction. To have a "heart of flesh" in contrast to a heart of stone is to be fully human in response to both God and creation.

170 From the Greek τάλαντον (measure or balance of scales) is a wooden board hammered in a distinct rhythmical pattern with two wooden hammers, used to call monks to prayer in Orthodox monasteries.

the heart awaiting our attention and presence in order to offer and receive the Holy Gifts.

Elder Aimilianos of Simonopetra Monastery suggests that the most important moment of the slow circular breathing that the holy neptic Fathers of the *Philokalia* speak of as characteristic of noetic prayer, is the silent stillness that occurs between the expiration and the next inhalation of breath. This brief moment of *hesychia* or stillness, waiting for the breath that revives and enlivens us, without which we cannot survive, is hardly ever even noticed. Like the food we eat every day, we take our breathing, its giftedness and the refreshment it gives, for granted, as we do our lives. Clement of Alexandria, the leader of the famous Christian catechetical school in Alexandria, Egypt in early part of the 2nd century, wrote in his *Miscellanies*, that we must seek to free ourselves from the ignorance of this mistake which he called "making the voluptuous choice."[171] We lack gratefulness, unaware that with each breath, we are breathing in God's name, Yaaahhh…Waaayyyy and the heart transmits it to every cell in our body of which our soul is an integral part. Without our conscious mindful awareness of the mystery taking place, this all happens in the background lacking our Grace-awakened gratitude.

Fr. John Romanides says that the spiritual heart transmits every part of the immaterial, invisible, noetically received divine Grace to the body. Whenever I am complacent or desire and grasp at the world without reference to God, I trade *dia-Logos* for monologos. At some point in beguilement, instead of (whispered in-breath) Yaaahhh… (whispered out-breath) Waaaaayyyy, Adam and Eve forgot about God and fascinated with life's voluptuousness, in effect shouted, as we have continued to do ever since, "Yeeeehaaaw!" as they became drunk with pleasure in the gifts of creation while becoming oblivious to the person of the Creator Who is hidden behind every particle of it. Slain by the giants of ignorance, forgetfulness, and laziness, like Esau who cared more for a bowl of soup than the father's blessing,

---

171 *Stromata* (Miscellanies), *Ante-Nicene Fathers*, Chapter 17, p. 627, Orthodox EBooks. The voluptuous choice is the taking of created life without reference to the Author of life. In other words, it is the loss of Eucharistic life and the fall into being subjugated to creation by our own desire for it.

they forfeited the vocation of their holy priesthood, exchanging vestments of Grace, for garments of skin. Failure to offer up one another and every moment of our whole lives to Christ our God, just as the priest does the bread and wine at the altar with the words, "Thine own of Thine own we offer Thee in all and for all" is the cause of our slavery to the passions that render our hearts hardened and unreceptive to the uncreated divine energies of Grace offered us.

Consciousness of the breath and being at the altar is a liturgy in which the other, whether person or the creation, communicates the presence of the Giver. But if we take the earth or even our spouse's body without our spouse, we have objectified him or her, divorcing him from the person and we end up with ashes. Christ in effect says to us in love, 'I am yours. I'm all in. Do with me whatever you want.' This is unfathomable in its full meaning. If all I wish, given the person of Christ, is to take the gifts He gives without Him, I have made the fatal mistake of making the voluptuous choice and I become a prisoner of that which I have grasped. My sin has subjected my being-in-the-Spirit to being captive to the created order. Instead of being the creation's priest and lifting it up to God for blessing to receive it back as a Eucharistic gift, I become its slave. The potential for being in the likeness of the uncreated One is revealed in the words from the Lord's prayer—"Thy will be done on earth as it is in heaven" (in the uncreated realm among the Holy Trinity)—is developmentally arrested and I am expelled from Paradise. So, Christ's passion-bearing is His willingness to be with us for all time in order that we may learn to breathe Him in consciously from the heart, with united body, soul, and mind as often as we re-member Him and are re-membered by Him. In this way, we become capable of responding to His love in the same way He offers Himself to us.

The same intention and hope in Christ that keeps us awake to the presence of God before partaking of creation, allows us to accompany others in their suffering, without dissociating as the Apostles did when faced with the Lord's agony in Gethsemane. A heart that can't break in grief is a heart that can't love. It is a heart that will never know real joy, because grief and joy both flow from the same depth. A heart of stone cannot give itself in love. If I want to take what God gives without God, I am swallowing the fatal poison the devil offers, which is to seek perfection without receiving it as a gift from the Only Lover of Humankind. Christ's perfection is revealed most truly through His mercy and sharing of our life in all its struggles, from birth to death, because He refuses to deny us freedom to return the love He offers us *by our own free choice*. The devil, by contrast, seeks perfection without mercy for anything or anyone else who is less than perfect. This leads to emptiness and despair.

Any part of creation that is not offered up to God for blessing before being received, is incapable of nourishing the soul. We begin to experience pain of spiritual starvation. Unless we wake up, we fall even further into delusion and captivity like every addict, seeking more and more of what can't satisfy us because it is only a reflection and not real. I am trying to satisfy myself with images of perfection and the pleasure they bring, while refusing to actually risk encountering the source of Life. There is no food tasty enough to heal the wound incurred by leaving God behind. There is no sexual delight that is good enough to transform the heart. Every imagined archetype pales in comparison to the joy of Christ. An old man and an old woman holding one another's hand and feeling the gratefulness and wonder that arise from sharing Christ together for 30 or 40 years, hurting one another, forgiving one another, loving one another, having an eye fall out and their hair rubbed off like *The Velveteen Rabbit*[172], tastes far more deeply of eros and joy than any carnal passions that can stimulate the body or the soul without the Spirit's participation. This quiet, invisible spiritual life our culture does not seem to recognize or value. Hollywood appears uninterested and perhaps incapable of showing it in the movies. It is closer to the humility and philanthropy of *philotimo*. About the time we begin to discover and taste its sweetness, like Abba Sisoes, we pass out of this life into the arms of Christ hoping for mercy, longing only for more time to repent and unable to adequately express our gratitude for the gift of life.

---

172   Margery Williams, New York: Doubleday, 1991.

The world is indeed voluptuous and good to look at and to touch, to be desired and enjoyed. God made it this way and on the seventh day from the *hesychia* of His own stillness and rest, He said of creation "It is very good." The problem of human suffering is found in the failure of humankind, the royal priesthood, to lift up every aspect of life for a blessing and become attentive to the Giver in receiving it. Apart from this we languish in the sleep of death entombed in our bodies, trapped behind self-protective monologues and carnal and vain desires of the heart of stone. "When eros for God has departed, together with the love of heavenly things and the hope of paradise, then the lust of the world, carnal pleasure, and diabolic deception come to rule a man."[173] Only face-to-face encounter with Christ standing at the door of our hearts and knocking, can save us from the joyless heart of stone and revive the heart of flesh in us. In repentance and humble recognition of our helplessness to change ourselves, we taste the Eucharistic joy offered us and are rendered immortal through participation in the infinite Divine Liturgy of love that is Christ.

> The body is called to become a liturgical body by interiorizing the celebration. The fundamental purpose of Orthodox ascesis and spirituality is to become aware of this rising body, sown by baptism inside the body and nourished by the Eucharist. For in its structure and its rhythms the human body is constituted to become "the temple of the Holy Spirit" as Paul says. This involves the two fundamental rhythms of respiration and of blood; and also the "space of the heart," a "space" which is both corporeal and spiritual.[174]

We are created to be in perpetual communion of intimacy with God and creation, offering up the world in a response of thanksgiving in return. "Every man is called to life in Him, that is, not only in

---

173   A Monk of Mount Athos, *The Watchful Mind.* Yonkers, NY: St. Vladimir's Seminary Press. 2014, p. 55.

174   Clement, Olivier, "Life in the Body" *The Ecumenical Review.* World Council of Churches. p. 135.

man's highest capacity for contemplation—his spirit—but in his feelings—his soul, and even his body."[175]

The implications of this potential for our care for one other and for creation that arises from continued prayer and repentance are profound. We do not grow less sensitive to embodied life as we grow in Grace, but more so. Elder Sophrony writes, "The Orthodox acetic does not wrestle with the body, but with passions and 'spiritual wickedness in high places' (Eph. 6:12.) for *it is not the body that keeps us from God—the body which is called to be the 'temple Holy Ghost, which is in you (1 Cor. 6:19) but the passions and their enjoyment.*[emphasis added]."[176] This greater sensitivity to life is from the place of the heart that communes with the Spirit and with created life and begins to care for the bodies of others, including all creation itself. In our fallen human condition, which is becoming increasingly accepted as "normal" in the world, we drastically underestimate how far we are from spiritual maturity that evidences such sensitivity.

Once when Elder Sophrony and his spiritual father, St. Silouan, were walking in the forests of Mt Athos, in a moment of inattention and distractedness, Fr. Sophrony pulled a leaf off of a tree. His spiritual mentor turned gently to him and said, "Your heart is not right." St. Silouan had begun to live in the Holy Spirit in such a way that he served at the altar of heart in continual prayer at all times and in all places. From his vantage point of humble obedience to the Spirit, every particle of creation deserved the respect and attention of being precious and a living testimony of divine love.[177] The earth and all its treasures and our own lives belong to us only to the degree that we have begun to offer everything first to God in prayer for a blessing, before partaking. This too is a reflection of what God is doing for creation. Prayer is noetic intercourse with the divine uncreated life, a perpetual thanksgiving to God who offers Himself in entirety

---

175   Sophrony, A. *Letters to His Family*, p.73.

176   Sophrony, A. *Truth and Life*. Essex, England: Stavropegic Monastery of St. John the Baptist, p. 99.

177   St. John Cassian writes that God is not only known through His incomprehensible noetic being, but "from the grandeur and beauty of his creatures." *Philokalia, Vol I*, p. 96.

to His creation most especially through the human heart in love and humility. The result of this "breathing" between the uncreated and created worlds is a continual repentance and humbling which leads to growth in love and mercy toward creation. "The more you to descend into the depths of the Spirit, the more you plumb the depths of humility. Correspondingly you gain greater knowledge of your own limitations and recognize the weakness of human nature; at the same time your love for God and your fellow beings waxes until you think that sanctification flows simply from a greeting or from the proximity of those with whom you live."[178]

We can see this reflected in the instructions of the hesychasts for preparation in prayer. They do not teach us to seek to leave our bodies in order to pray, but to enter more deeply within them, by drawing the *nous*[179] inside the body in order to be grounded in our actual existence rather than allowing our mind to be disembodied by occupying our imagination or identified with the object of our senses instead. In his *Three Methods of Prayer* St. Simeon the New Theologian instructs beginners to "focus your physical gaze, together with the whole of your intellect (*nous*), upon the center of your belly or your navel" and having made this mind-body unifying intention and collected attention, then "search inside yourself with your intellect (*nous*) so as to find the place of the heart."[180]

There is a subtle but quite distinct difference in the 'taste' between the mind being dispersed through the senses without attentiveness and when it is being drawn back into the body through mindfulness. When the mind is not actively present collecting itself and drawing the senses within the body in silence and inwardly alert stillness, automaticity and distraction hold sway. Reactivity of the affective and instinctive centers of the body are drawn into action as the attention is captured by various objects of the imagination or the

---

178   St. Niketas Stethatos, *Philokalia Vol IV*, pp. 117–118.

179   A Greek word denoting the contemplative mind in distinction to the reasoning, thinking mind. The *nous* is considered by the Holy Fathers as the "eye" of the heart through which noetic revelation comes and illumines the whole body and the feelings.

180   *Philokalia Vol. IV*, pp. 338–339.

senses, without mindful awareness of this taking place. By contrast, when the senses are drawn in by the *nous*, and apprehended from the heart, a new quality of collected attention, consciously aware of itself, arises which is referred to by the Fathers as "guarding of the heart." This condition of watchfulness involves noticing the movements of the imagination, the senses, and the feelings, from deep within, without automatically being captured by them, in order to concentrate on praying without distraction. While this naturally happens when compunction arises, it requires an inner effort that must be constantly renewed until Grace warms the heart and attracts its attention with love. Isaac the Syrian points to the important distinction between "attracted" attention which is automatically dispersed through the senses and attention which is intentionally used to draw the mind within the body, noting that this makes a significant difference in the quality of nourishment received by the soul. "Whenever the mind is drawn away by the senses, it also eats the food of beasts with them. But when the senses are drawn by the mind, they partake together with it of the sustenance of angels."[181]

St. Gregory Palamas counsels the same thing in his defense of the practice of the hesychasts of drawing the mind inside the body as the foundation for prayer in his debates with Barlaam. "It is necessary to bring the *nous* back and enclose it within the body and particularly within that innermost body, within the body that we call the heart."[182] Encountering the divine *nous* in this way, Palamas teaches, "the body that is attached to the *nous* is refashioned by the *nous* into something more divine."[183] By contrast, when the body and *nous* are not connected mindfully in this way, with conscious intention of standing before Christ, the divine energies of Grace are prevented from reaching the heart because of its fragmented, disembodied state. St. Mark the Ascetic characterized this state as being one in which the

181   St. Isaac the Syrian, *The Ascetical Homilies.* p. 144.

182   *Philokalia*, Vol. IV, p. 334.

183   From "Defense of the Hesychasts" 1.3.33. cited in Keselopoulos, (2004) A. *Passions and Virtues According to Saint Gregory Palamas*. South Canaan, Pennsylvania: *St.* Tikhon's Seminary Press: p. 192.

"three giants of "ignorance, forgetfulness, and laziness" prevent access to the heart.

It is also clear that these instructions do not refer to mere "navel gazing" as Barlaam suggested in his debates with St. Gregory Palamas, or as some modern voices have suggested, reducing prayer to a technical method, as though a technique of mindfulness alone could transform us into the likeness of God. Only the gift of Divine Grace can do that. Rather, the holy neptic Fathers knew that prayer begins from a foundation of embodiment and repentance in the real presence-in-the-moment of our lives; down to earth, humble. We stand (or bow or kneel) before God 'just as I am' without image or artifice, in grateful self-offering. Prayer does not use imagination nor do we search for high states of illumination described by the saints like the Apostle Paul who in *theoria* of noetic prayer declares "whether in the body or not I do not know." These advanced states are under the direction of the Holy Spirit who cries out within us, "Abba, Father!"[184] and teach themselves. They are part of the divine mystery and a gift of the divine will to humble and contrite hearts.

For us who are beginners, the proper foundation for prayer is one of simplicity in faith and love that begins in sobriety, humbly, close to the earth without illusions. Even this is not so easy for a generation glued to iPhones, computer screens, and televisions who find it difficult to go a minute without craving the stimulation of more information and content and who want instant gratification. In this way, we are continually drawn back into our *dianoia*, our discursive reasoning, and out through our senses in search of the world as an object of stimulation, rather than by drawing the *nous* into the body and creating a space where we can stop and be poised at the altar, let go of the world, offer it up for blessing and receive it back with thanksgiving as a bearer of Grace. Lord, let me be loved by You through my spouse and through the apple I eat, through the sand I walk on, and the sound of the birds I hear. Let me be loved by You. It is You Lord Who are the source of all, in all and Whom I wish to receive. If I want You, then I will receive my wife as a most precious co-pilgrim

---

184 Gal. 4:6.

and notice the bird's song as an angelic herald. Everything becomes a testimony of the divine presence and purpose underlying all things. But if I seek anything other than You in the world, I lose everything else as well becoming a slave to my own merciless craving. Offering everything to Christ and seeking Him through all, frees creation to be revealed beyond our projections. Without becoming aware of the proverbial "log in my eye" (which is my entire experience) the "between" necessary for communion collapses into the monologue of objectification of the other who is judged according to my experience. If I am to encounter the created order and other persons iconically as revelations of God's presence, then I must approach everything and everyone through Christ who is "between" us. Bowing in *metanoia* before Christ is necessary in order to encounter an 'other' than myself beyond my projections. All real meeting is *dia-Logos*.

Prayer does not exist where there is no encounter with an *other* whose value makes an ethical and existential demand on me. I cannot merely pass by the *face* of the other on my way to worship or prayer, as the priest and the Levite did the wounded man in the ditch,[185] nor continue harboring in my heart unforgiveness. Attention in daily life, repentance, forgiveness, and self-offering love are essential aspects of prayer otherwise we are fooling ourselves. When St. Gregory Palamas says, "If someone only wants to pray when he attends God's Church, and has no concern at all for prayer at home, in the streets or in the fields, then even when he is present in church he is not really praying." he helps us realize that we do not go to the Holy Communion at the altar of the Divine Liturgy without going forth to the altar of the heart of my neighbor in daily life. These two encounters are one. "Behold I approach Christ our Immortal King and God." I receive Him into me and He receives me into Him. When I turn around, I have already walked through the door and now the least of these and the greatest of these, I stand before as the Apostle Thomas did the Risen Lord, with only one possible question. You look like an ordinary group of people except that Christ has received you into Him and shines through you. What is

---

185 Lk. 10:25–37

it that moves me from an ordinary world in which I view everything from my limited human experience to determine each one's value, to one in which, like Thomas, my heart noetically awakens to recognize "My Lord and my God" in the face of each person I see? The only proper response to you who have been taken up into Christ, is in my heart to fall on my face in repentance before the Lord. Christ is between each of us, loving through us and we are each being loved by Him through one another.[186] Without recognizing Christ among us in this way, there is only the monologue of my projections on to others which assimilates them according to my experience. According to a saying attributed to the *Talmud*, "We do not see the world as it is but as we are." We depend on noetic encounter with Christ through the Holy Spirit that is beyond psychology in order to be transformed and enter into real relationship with others and with Creation. In order to have an actual relationship with others, I must meet each one of them in and through Christ and receive Christ through them.

This involves a gradual and total conversion of our lives to Christ[187] that affects every aspect of it. It involves a change in our response to culture and the assumptions of the time and place in which we live which subtly affects how we see the world, often without us realizing it. Fr. Alexander Schmemann points out:

> There is no point in converting people to Christ if they do not convert their vision of the world and of life, since Christ becomes merely a symbol for all that we live and want already—without Him. This kind of Christianity is more terrifying than agnosticism or hedonism.[188]

---

186   Fr. Dumitru Staniloae writes, "Working spiritually (with love for Him) in myself I awake the others love to Him, which has been awakened by the influence of His love for them. Christ loves me through all, they love me too together and I love them, with Christ, as well as Christ loves them through me" *Liturghia comunității și jertfa interioară în viziunea filocalică.* (trans. by Rev. Konstantinos Karaisaridis, into Greek *I poreia me ton Sotira Christo*) trans. to English by Vasileios Thermos, *Walking with Christ the Savior*, Greece: To Perivoli Tis Panaghias, 1984, p. 89.

187   This is the fulfillment of the litany chanted repeatedly by the deacon in the Divine Liturgy "Let us commit ourselves and one another and our whole life to Christ our God."

188   Alexander Schmemann, *The Journals of Father Alexander Schmemann*

Gradually, we need to discover, like the Apostles outside the Garden of Gethsemane, how we go to sleep again and again before the pain of the human condition, when the Lord is inviting us to stay neptically awake with Him. We need to see how puny is our love and care for others, to realize how much we are dominated by the little tyrants of pleasure and pain, like and dislike, and how much we take for granted, how little gratefulness and response-ability we have for the privilege of living at any given moment.

Full human potential is measured by Christ who is beyond reckoning. Prayer is the most difficult action of all; the longest waiting, the deepest emptiness, the greatest helplessness—a single-minded vulnerability hoping for the heart to be set on fire by the unseen noetic flame that heralds the advance of the King of Glory. God wishes to commune with Creation through humanity and offers Himself entirely to make this possible. In effect, when God says to us in Christ, as the only lover of humankind, 'I am yours do with Me whatever you want.' He knows that this will be costly. But He hopes in us, that moved by this love and in His image over a lifetime, we will mature into persons willing to return to Him the same offering, as Abraham, Isaac, Jacob, Job, the Holy Theotokos, Apostles and martyrs have done, saying to God in response with their whole lives, "I am yours. Do with me whatever you want. I trust myself to Your care whether I am ill, alone, unrecognized, slandered or unjustly treated."

Childlike fervent prayer in faith and obedience to the divine will gradually awaken conscience. The choices we make based on the small moments of prayer and inner wakefulness throughout each day, are most important and constitute our response to the divine proposal of marriage with Christ our God. When we are in love, the beloved is constantly in mind and all our actions are arranged in response to this love relationship. No sacrifice is too great. The love of God for humankind is revealed in Christ's willingness to go to hell for the sake of His beloved. The only possible response worthy of such love is to offer ourselves in the same way in return, to go to

---

1973–1983 trans. Juliana Schmemann, Crestwood, NY: St. Vladimir's Seminary Press, 2002, p. 17.

hell for the sake of the Beloved and all whom He loves. This willingness is the sign of those who bear the marks of Grace received in prayer and love, even for one's enemies, as St. Silouan has reminded us. Those who have tasted Grace have entered the lion's den and sought to stand fast before what they encountered and wrestle with the powers and principalities that tempt man to doubt that there is any meaning to human struggle. Those who stand fast to the end learn the depth of meaning which Fr. Ernesto Cardenal captures so well. "We are born with aching hearts, as the heart of Jesus was also pierced. We are not a meaningless passion as Sartre calls us, but a passion whose meaning is God.[189]

At the heart of it all we search for Christ and the question before us at any moment, has to do with which of the two paths we choose. If we seek Christ, the world becomes itself as God intended in all His joy and love. If I only want Creation without the Creator, and make the voluptuous choice without reference to God, I am opening the door to hell. Christ knows that we will struggle with this and He waits for us to realize our mistake in order, like the breath of life, to come rushing back to us, conquering the death we bring upon ourselves, by dying with us and transforming even hell with His mercy. Glory be to Thee O Lord.

---

189 *Love: A Glimpse of Eternity*, Massachusetts: Paraclete Press, 2006, p. 20.

PART II

The Holy Fathers called prayer the queen of virtues, for it attracts virtues too. But the higher
it is, the more work it requires. St. Agathon
says: Prayer is warfare to the last breath.[190]

Behold the Faith which Christ Gave,
The Apostles Preached, And the Fathers Preserved!

---

190 John, Fr., *Christ Is In Our Midst: Letters from a Russian Monk,* Crestwood,
NY: St. Vladimir's Seminary Press, 1980, p. 2.

Chapter 6

ON THE RELATIONSHIP BETWEEN THE BODY AND NOETIC PRAYER OF THE HEART[191]

Those who hold forth about spiritual realities without hav-ing tasted and experienced them are like a man traversing an empty and arid plain at high noon on a summer's day; in his great and burning thirst he imagines that there is a cool spring close at hand, full of sweet clear water, and that there is nothing to prevent him from drinking it to his heart's content. Or they are like man who, without having tasted a drop of honey, tries to explain to others what its sweetness is like. Such indeed are those who try to introduce others to perfection, sanctity and dispassion without having learnt about these things through their own efforts and direct expe-rience. Had God given them even a slight awareness of the things about which they speak, they would see that the truth about them differs greatly from the explanation that they give. Christianity is liable to be misconstrued little by little in this way, and so turned into atheism... These things are not to be understood merely in a theoretical way; they must be achieved within the mind in a mysterious manner through the activity of the Holy Spirit, and only then can they be spoken about.[192]

—St. Macarios of Egypt

---

191 This is an edited and expanded version of a personal letter to an Athonite hieromonk who knows the Holy Fathers well and whose genuine and sober ques-tions I greatly value. I have developed it further as a literary device to summarize the neptic Tradition as it relates to prayer and embodiment as an invitation and encouragement to readers to explore the riches of these witnesses concerning the deep things of prayer.

192 Palmer, Sherrard and Ware, (Eds.) *The Philokalia*, Vol. III, London: Faber & Faber, 1984. p. 320.

Dear Father,

I should be wiser than to try and respond to questions about noetic prayer since I am clearly a beginner and know very little. *Caveat emptor* applies to everything I say. I can only speak of what I have read from others and been taught myself and practiced poorly for the last 40 years making very small progress. Yet without the little bit of effort I have made overshadowed by the unmerited Grace of God I cannot imagine how my life might have been. Even with my poor stumblings and weakness, I am grateful to God in His mercy for bringing me out of my ignorance, forgetfulness, and laziness, again and again, and blessing me with renewed joy and hope as a balm for the sorrow at my helplessness to change myself. I can only cling to God and place in Him the hope of my salvation.

I do not know if I am imagining things in some way that makes me only think my heart is warming to the Lord. I do not know if my meager and rare few moments of tears are more than self-indulgence and imagination. All I can say is that when I read the prayers for Holy Communion or the confessions of St. Peter Damascus in the *Philokalia*, I am comforted knowing that all the sins apply to me, so at least I am not totally deluded. Lord have mercy on me for daring to respond to you and also protect you from being influenced by my presumption and naiveté. In hopeful sincerity and love, and with desire that God or others who know better will in love correct my errors, drawing on the Holy Fathers, I will say only the little I can that seems to have been helpful to me and for which I remain deeply grateful to my first teacher of stillness and the embodied life of watchfulness. And also to Elder Ephraim of Philotheou who long ago confirmed that the embodied attention I had learned to practice, was true to what he had learned from his experience on the Holy Mountain and he gave his blessing for me to continue, while seeking to pray the Jesus prayer from the heart.

I cannot claim to speak of the deeper things of prayer. The Holy Spirit is the teacher of this dimension of noetic prayer. I will only speak of the value of striving to have a "collected presence" that, in conjunction with faith, is a preparatory foundation for noetic prayer of the heart. Repentance and tears of compunction whenever these occur, even for the briefest of moments, are always accompanied by such collected presence that happens naturally. Mind and body are united and the heart communicates to the whole being what it discovers noetically, without even comprehending how. I will try to say something about the preparation for noetic prayer which involves stillness and watchfulness in a fully embodied, collected state.

You say even in the monastery you lack adequate time for the prayer. From what you describe, it seems to me that you could begin by trimming another half an hour off your waking cycle. Elder Ephraim of Katounakia said that if we will faithfully give prayer of inner stillness and collected attention 30 minutes a day, it will be enough to begin to draw us deeper into longer periods gradually through increasing desire for it.[193] He thought this was the minimum time daily necessary for this to occur. Others, like St. Porphyrios say that even five minutes of simple heartfelt love and devotion is worth more than hours of time spent without this. Though these instructions may sound contradictory on the surface, Archimandrite Sophrony's counsel remains true. Regardless of what kind of practice we are involved in, (and the approach to prayer differs among personality types, circumstances and needs of persons which is why it is desirable to have a good spiritual father or mother who is experienced and knows us well) we do not come to Christ through being forced, but only with a willing, yearning heart out of love. Prayer cannot be reduced to a set of techniques or an action we can do on our own power, but is always a response to the gift of divine Grace that has awakened this desire for the unseen God in us, however dimly felt. Met. Anthony Bloom said that in Christianity, all psychophysiological exercises related to breath, posture, attention and such, *"originated from the Fathers observing what happened to them when they were in a state of prayer."*[194] The whole point of seeking to follow any of these instructions is to help render us vulnerable to the actions of divine Grace, although in and of themselves, they are neither the cause nor a guarantee of it.

---

193   Ephraim, E. *Elder Ephraim of Katounakia.* (trans. T. Vassiliadou-Christodoulou), Mt. Athos, Greece: H. Hesychasterion "Saint Ephraim", p. 224.
194   Needleman, J. p. 37.

St. Isaac the Syrian counsels that if we seek inner prayer of the heart we should begin by forcing "ourselves to be silent and then from out of this silence something is born that leads us into silence itself."[195] A certain kind of "force" or immovability of *thymos* (incensive desire) and *epithymia* (eros/wish) are needed to support and hold still the *nous* (mind) inside the body and keep re-directing it to the place of the heart so that such willingness can grow. Just as in any relationship of depth and intimacy, without a high quality of attention in a recollected state of presence, we can't really expect much. And yet, at the heart of prayer is love, which cannot ever be forced. As St. Isaac the Syrian explains, "so long as a man makes efforts, striving to force the spiritual to come down to him, it resists."[196] Love makes for the highest quality of attention and is "the rightful door leading to contemplation."[197] Often we do not feel the warmth of heart that comes from love and it is at such times that we must make an effort to concentrate. Elder Sophrony describes the Christian's state of inner activity in prayer and watchfulness as being "like a high-tension cable on which a little bird can perch without the least harm, yet through which passes an energy capable of blowing up the whole world. This is how we will gain entry to the eternal kingdom of Christ."[198]

In this collected state of presence, we wait to "catch the wind" of the Spirit that blows upon us by being still enough to notice the sheer silence of *presence*, like Elijah in the cave,[199] beneath the clamor and thunderings of our attention which is constantly distracted and often "captured" by the coarse instinctive cravings, emotional imaginings and the mechanical wanderings of our unguarded intellect. Lest we fall to thinking we can follow some kind of prescribed method to our destination, we do well to recall Martin Laird's instructive

---

195   Homily 64 *The Ascetical Homilies of St. Isaac the Syrian*, Holy Transfiguration Monastery.

196   "Directions on Spiritual Training," *Early Fathers form the Philokalia*, 150., p. 228.

197   Ibid, 149., p. 227.

198   *Words of Life* (Essex: Stavropegic Monastery of St. John the Baptist, 1996) pp. 37–38.

199   1 Kings 19:12.

description of the way to approach noetic prayer of the heart. "There is no way into the silence except surrender and there is no map of the silence that is surrender."[200] This is congruent with the insights of Fr. Georges Florovsky, one of my professors, who wrote, "Christianity does not give us a map but a key to the Kingdom of Heaven. We may get lost, but whatever we find will be real." In other words, we can't accomplish prayer by simply making ourselves "do" silence as a form of individual meditation. Something much greater is needed, and that is love. Even more so, what Fr. Florovsky says about our approach to the holy Scriptures also applies to prayer. "No one profits by the Gospels unless he be first in love with Christ. For Christ is not a text but a living Person, and He abides in His Body, the Church."[201]

When asked about prayer by a beginning monk, the illumined Romanian Elder Cleopas of Sihastria answered simply by quoting the words of St. Paul, *Pray without ceasing!*[202] day and night until you feel the grace of the Holy Spirit in your heart."[203] To another more experienced monk he answered in more detail, but still briefly. "First, pray with your voice, with words; prayer will then move from the mouth to the mind and finally to the heart. But this requires much effort, a fountain of tears and the grace of the Holy Spirit."[204] As an interior act of our spirit, Elder Sophrony points out that words are not always necessary; prayer is often expressed in silence. "We remain silent because God sees all the depth of our thought, all the longing of our heart, and we are not always capable of expressing them in words. But God understands the secret movements of our heart and responds to them."[205] The very effort of any egocentric doing may

---

200   Martin Laird, Into *the Silent Land: A Guide to the Christian Practice of Contemplation* Oxford University Press: England, 2006, p. 3.

201   Florovsky, G. (1987). *Bible, church, tradition: An Eastern Orthodox View,* (Volume 1 in the *Collected Works of Georges Florovsky*). Belmont, MA: Nordland Publishing. p. 14.

202   I Thess. 5:17.

203   Balan, Ioanichie, *Elder Cleopa of Sihastria,* Lake George, CO: New Varatec Publishing, 2001, p. 220.

204   Ibid.

205   Sophrony, A. *Letters To his Family,* Essex, England: Stavropegic Monastery of St. john the Baptist, 2015, p. 69.

even disturb the silence and interfere with the reception of Grace. Doing something can be a kind of distraction in and of itself if it is not a response to love. When the rich young ruler asked Christ what else he could do to become perfect, Christ responded by saying in effect, "Let go of all you have collected by your own power and efforts, which you are now attached to, so you can simply follow me." His invitation brought to the surface a conflict in the young man whose heart was divided along the fault line that separates the search for worldly *kenodoxia* from the response to heavenly *orthodoxia* of the divine energies of unmerited Grace. Such an invitation of love at the moment was too decisive a cutting of the egoistic will and pride of self-sufficiency for this man.

Unless we are repeatedly defeated in our efforts to be still apart from love, we are not likely to discover the stillness that is effortless which comes from surrender in love to the Spirit's initiative. Or if we do, we fail to truly value and protect it as divine gift from beyond our own doing because we lack sufficient experience of our own failures to bring this about on our own. Humility is needed and we begin to acquire this through our struggle and failures. Elder Ephraim of Katounakia writes, "Humility comes from obedience and prayer and the humbler a man makes himself the more he approaches God and the more sinful he considers himself. Thus, he cries and laments and asks for God's mercy. Needless to say, he considers everyone else saints and angels."[206]

Such humility is taught only by the wrestle to become obedient to what prayer reveals in the heart. There is no progress in prayer without progress in obedience which brings humility that distinguishes human effort from divine help. And this comes only as we learn in practice to call on the Lord with fervor and not depend on ourselves or attribute any apparent progress in prayer to our own doings. St. Isaac the Syrian counsels,

> As soon as a man realizes his weakness and genuinely
> feels it, he at once rouses his soul from indolence and
> becomes cautious. But no one can feel his weakness

---

206 Ephraim, E. p. 314.

unless even a small temptation, either of body or soul, is allowed to assail him—and he is granted deliverance from it. For then he sees clearly the futility of his own efforts and measures, he sees that the circumspection, abstinence and guarding of his soul, through which he hoped to find security, brought him no profit and that deliverance came independently of it all. Hence he is shown that by himself he is nothing and is saved by God's help alone.[207]

The struggle with temptation is part of the school of prayer in which obedience and failure lead to humility, practical wisdom and increase our trust in God and the desire for prayer.

As soon as you awaken in the morning, after having slept, your mind will be optimally ready for being attentive. If you use the prayer bench, situate yourself as we discussed and spend a few minutes making sure you establish a good grounded, mind-body unity because as St. Mark the Ascetic says, "When our mind and flesh are not in union, our state deteriorates."[208] St. Mark also instructs us to be physically still in every part of the body for as he explains, "the intellect cannot be still unless the body is still."[209] Let there be no movement at all. Relaxed. Alert. This requires attention and intention, but it is well worth the effort, for as St. Macarios of Egypt affirms, "Understanding cannot enter you unless you practice stillness."[210]

Of course I need not remind you that prayer is not simply relaxation or merely the sensual rest of a "Calgon bath"[211] as many

---

207 Kadloubovsky and Palmer, (eds) *Early Fathers from the Philokalia*, London: Faber & Faber, 1976, p. 249.

208 Text from G.E.H. Palmer, Philip Sherrard, and Kallistos Ware (trans. and eds.) The Philokalia: The Complete Text, vol. I (Faber & Faber, London & Boston: 1979), 46. pp. 129.

209 Palmer, G.E.H., Sherrard, P. and Ware, K. *Philokalia Vol I,* London: Faber & Faber. (1979) P128

210 From "The first Syriac Epistle", Appendix B, *The Ascetical Homilies of Saint Isaac the Syrian,* Holy Transfiguration Monastery, Boston, Massachusetts, 2011. P. 160.

211 Reference to an old television commercial depicting a sensual aromatic bath using Calgon products where the woman says "Calgon, take me away…" from the stress.

connoisseurs of psychic self-calming settle for these days. While this can clearly be healthful and a relief from stress, it is merely physically and psychologically beneficial, but in and of itself, not spiritual. In preparing for prayer, there is a definite intentionality and alert attention that must be renewed again and again, as we seek the more interior place of the heart. All three powers of the soul must be collected and working in harmony. This is said to occur when the "concupiscible part desires virtue, the irascible does battle for it, and the rational devotes itself to a contemplation of the created."[212]

Then with the mind guarding the heart, it is possible to be aware of what is happening both with the energies of the body and the thoughts and inclinations. St. Gregory Palamas points out that "in prayer, the *nous* is obliged to watch over the complete man, body and soul. Thus, the observation and continuous surveillance of the *nous* in these two domains is absolutely vital if man is to be delivered from the various passions of his soul and body"[213] that impede responsiveness to Grace. Elder Zacharias of Essex points to the unity of mind, body and soul that is involved in the biblical understanding of heart. "We are sustained by a living sensation of God in our hearts, in our bodies. That is why the Old Testament asks, 'What is man?' (Job 7:17, Ps. 8:4; 144:3) And the answer is given in the Proverbs: 'Man is a heart with a divine and spiritual sensation.' (Prov. 15:14 [LXX]) that is to say, a man who bears in his heart the traces of God's energy, of God's presence, of the effects of Grace.[214]

From the place of the heart, which is understood to be both physical and non-physical, an organ existing "between two worlds" and capable of receiving the infusion of divine noetic energies of Grace, it is possible to become aware of something that is beyond individual sensations and thoughts and begins to move beyond the borders of space and time. Without even realizing how, Elder Sophrony

212　Evagrius Ponticus, cited in Bunge, G. p. 15.

213　From Defense of the Hesychasts 1.2.9 cited in Keselopoulos, (2004) A. *Passions and Virtues According to Saint Gregory Palamas. St.* Tikhon's Seminary Press: South Canaan, Pennsylvania, p. 160.

214　Archimandrite Zacharias, *Remember Thy First Love: The Three Stages of the Spiritual Life in the Theology of Elder Sophrony.* Mount Thabor Publishing: Pennsylvania, 2010, p. 353.

explains, through the collected attention of faith receptive to the divine energies of Grace,

> eventually the mind sees not the physical heart, but that
> which is happening within it—the feelings that creep
> in and the mental images that approach from without...
> When the attention of the mind is fixed in the heart it
> is possible to control what happens in the heart, and the
> battle against passions assumes a rational character. The
> enemy is recognized and can be driven off by the power
> of the Name of Christ... The heart becomes so highly
> sensitive, so discerning that eventually when praying for
> anyone the heart can tell almost at once the state of the
> person prayed for.[215]

Jesus says "Behold I stand at the door [of the heart] and knock. If anyone should hear my voice and open the door, then I will come in and dine with him and he with Me."[216] But how do we open the door to the heart?

In his *Three Methods of Prayer* St. Simeon the New Theologian directs to "focus your physical gaze, together with the whole of your intellect (*nous*), upon the center of your belly or your navel" and having made this mind-body unifying intention and collected attention, then "search inside yourself with your intellect (*nous*) so as to find the place of the heart."[217] St. John Climacus describes the hesychast's intention as striving "to confine his incorporeal being within his bodily house, paradoxical as this is."[218] St. Gregory Palamas counsels the same in defending this continuing practice of drawing the mind inside the body as the foundation for prayer in his debates with Barlaam. "It is necessary to bring the *nous* back and enclose it within the

---

215   Sophrony, A. (1977) *His Life Is Mine*, trans. Rosemary Edmonds, Crestwood, NY: St. Vladimir's, p. 14.

216   Rev. 3:20.

217   *Philokalia, Vol. IV*, pp. 338–339.

218   St. John Climacus, *The Ladder of Divine Ascent* (1959) p. 237.

body and particularly within that innermost body, within the body, that we call the heart."[219]

Commenting on this statement, Archbishop Chrysostomos explains:

> The body, he reminds us, must participate actively in prayer, facilitating the return of the mind to the heart. The concentration of the mind, in silence and stillness, on the center of the body (the navel) and the consequent removal of distractions during the recitation of the Jesus prayer, St. Gregory says, in response to Barlaam's accusation of *omphaloskopia* (navel-gazing)—or corollary proclamations that the Athonite hesychasts were "*omphalopsychoi*" (from the Greek words for "navel" and "soul"), or individuals who believed that the soul resided in the navel—are 'aids' in returning the mind to the heart and achieving the knowledge of God which is contained therein. Moreover, through this kind of psychosomatic concentration, the hesychasts are able to achieve a profound level of prayer—*prayer of the heart*—that leads to the integration of thought and spiritual knowledge, enlightening the mind and bringing the body and soul into perfect harmony.[220]

St. Niketas Stethatos writes, "The unconfused union and conjunction of soul and body constitutes, when maintained in harmony, a single reality, whether on the visible level or in their inner being."[221] Of course, prayer of the heart is in its essence, communion with Christ who is love. This alone heals the human condition and transforms us into the likeness of the One with whom we commune, for

---

219 *Philokalia, Vol. IV,* p. 334.
220 Chrysostomos, A. *A Guide to Orthodox Psychotherapy: The Science, Theology and Spiritual Practice Behind It and Its Clinical Application,* University Press of America, 2007, pp. 81–82.
221 "On Spiritual Knowledge, 93. *Philokalia Vol. IV,* p. 170.

as St. Maximos the Confessor observes, "Only love overcomes the fragmentation of human nature."[222]

Watchfulness (νῆψις) in prayer consists not only of attentiveness of soul but also of attentiveness of bodily sensation as a part of standing guard at the door of the heart. St. John Chrysostom explains: "When an archer desires to shoot his arrows successfully, he first takes great pains over his posture and aligns himself accurately with his mark. It should be the same for you who are about to shoot the head of the wicked devil. Let us be concerned first for the good order of sensations and then for the good posture of inner thoughts."[223] In the same vein, Elder Ephraim of Philotheou defined watchfulness as "attention to thoughts, fantasies, *and the movements of the senses* [emphasis added]."[224]

In his teachings on the hesychastic method of prayer, St. Gregory Palamas was emphatic about the relationship between soul and body in prayer and watchfulness:

> When, then, someone is striving to concentrate his intellect in himself so that it functions, not according to the direct form of movement but according to the circular, delusion-free form, how could he not gain immensely if instead of letting his gaze flit hither and thither, he fixes it upon his chest or his navel as upon a point of support? ... 'Be attentive to yourself,' says Moses (Deut. 15:9. LXX) - that is, to the whole of yourself, not to a few things that pertain to you, neglecting the rest. By what means? With the intellect assuredly, for nothing else can pay attention to the whole of yourself. Set this guard, therefore, over your soul and body, for thereby you will readily free yourself from the evil passions of body and soul. Take yourself in hand, then, be attentive

---

222 *Centuries on Love* PG 91, 396, Cited in Clement, Olivier *The Roots of Christian Mysticism: Texts from the Patristic Era with Commentary.* New City Press: New York, 1993, p. 136.

223 PG 48:734 (As translated in: *The Monastic Rule of Iosif Volotsky*, p. 125).

224 *Counsels from the Holy Mountain,* Florence: AZ: St. Anthony's Monastery, 1999, p. 315.

to yourself, scrutinize yourself; or, rather, guard, watch over and test yourself, for in this manner you will subdue your rebellious unregenerate self to the Spirit and there will never again be 'some secret iniquity in your heart' (Deut. 15:9). If, says, the Preacher, the spirit that rules over the evil demons and passions rises up against you, do not desert your place (cf., Eccles. 10:4)—that is to say, *do not leave any part of your soul or body unwatched* [emphasis added]. In this way you will master the evil spirits that assail you and you will boldly present yourself to Him who examines hearts and minds (cf. Ps. 7:9); and He will not scrutinize you, for you will have already scrutinized yourself. As St. Paul says, 'If we judged ourselves we would not be judged' (1 Cor. 11:31).[225]

It is clear that this paradoxical effort of collected, embodied attention is not accurately construed as "navel gazing" as Barlaam suggested, as though a technique of mere mind-body unity in and of itself was able to transform us. Nor is it simply an awareness of sensation for its own sake. Rather, this collected, mind-embodied state is a foundation for keeping watch over and purifying the senses while decreasing distraction by drawing the mind within the body and deeper still into the body of the heart.

In this sense, embodied prayer is seen to be an extension of receiving Christ through Holy Communion as is found in the prayer of St. Symeon Metaphrastes who asks for Christ to be drawn within the members of his body. "O my Maker, pass through me for the right ordering of my members, into all my joints, my reins,[226] and my heart. Burn up the thorns of all mine offence. Purify my soul: sanctify my mind, make firm my knees and bones. Enlighten the simple unity of my five senses.[227] Similarly, the body is purified noetically in prayer, as St. Hesychius the priest explains, when the senses are guarded, as

225 *The Philokalia, Volume IV*, London: Faber and Faber, 1995, pp. 338–339.
226 "Reins" is used by the Fathers to refer to the passionate part of the soul (thymos and epithymia).
227 Prayer after Holy Communion, *Prayer Book for Orthodox Christians*. Holy Transfiguration Monastery: Boston, p. 357.

it were, with an intentional active mindfulness, rather than serving as outlets for the dispersal of a distracted attention. "An intellect that does not neglect its inner struggle will find that the five bodily senses, too, are freed from all external evil influences. It withdraws the senses almost completely into itself."[228] St. Niketas Stethatos, a disciple of St. Symeon the New Theologian, speaks of this same refinement of the senses that happens through inner collectedness:

> If you refer the activities of the outer senses back to their inner counterparts—exposing your sight to the intellect, the beholder of the light of life, your hearing to the judgment of the soul, your taste to the discrimination of the intelligence, your sense of smell to the understanding of the intellect, and relating your sense of touch to the watchfulness of the heart—you will lead an angelic life on earth; while being and appearing as a man among men, you will also be an angel coexisting with angels and spiritually conscious in the same way as they are.[229]

It is quite likely that the monastic strugglers and ancient hesychasts for centuries lived a more normal and embodied presence not divorced from the created order of which they were a part. It is from this more natural physical connection with the Creation, that they sought to sustain a quality of collected attention. Modern people, especially those of us in the world, cannot take for granted that we have the same relationship to our essential embodied selves and the natural world as the holy Fathers did or that we begin from the same starting place as a result, due to the artificiality of our lives. We also live much more physically comfortable and digitally distracted lives and are not used to the intensity of confrontation with stark realities of our mortal condition. Elder Sophrony says

> What monks acquired after decades of weeping, our contemporaries think to receive after a brief

---

228 *Philokalia*, Vol. 1, 53. On watchfulness and holiness, pp. 171–172.
229 *Philokalia*, Vol IV, pp. 80–81.

interval—sometimes even in a few hours of pleasant "theological" discussion. Christ's words—His every word—came to this world from on High. They belong to a sphere of other dimensions and can be assimilated only by means of prolonged prayer with much weeping. Otherwise, they will continue incomprehensible to man, however "educated" he be, even theologically.[230]

Our inner weakness, spiritual naiveté and the loss of natural embodied presence all can lead to subtle confusions easily overlooked. Olivier Clement observes,

People in the west are today so uptight, tense, nervous, confined to the surface of life that they need to calm themselves and to go more deeply into the meaning of the body and of the poetry of things before approaching traditional ascetic practices. These are designed for people of ancient cultures, cultures of silence and a slow pace.[231]

By contrast, we moderns have become drawn into our disembodied imaginations and *personalities*, hypnotized by television, artificial environments and captivity of our attention to ubiquitous digital media, so that we exist in more of a hypnotic fascination, dissociated from our bodies, much of the time. The earth, its creatures and one another are depersonalized and reduced to commodities and information—"things" from which we expect to extract a profit or produce a benefit, rather than relate with as living beings with an intrinsic value expressing the divine joy and as "treasures in earthen vessels."

We exist in a state of perpetual spiritual beguilement, often lost in our imaginations in contrast to direct mindful connection with the sensation of our own bodies and the earth of which we are a part. Ironically it is our beguilement by the passions in this way that

---

230   Sophrony, A. *On Prayer*, Crestwood, NY: St. Vladimir's Seminary Press, 1996, p. 92.

231   Clement, Olivier, "Life in the Body" *The Ecumenical Review*. World Council of Churches. p. 137.

renders us less sensitive. The irony of modern existence is that our self-indulgence and unrecognized slavery to the hypnosis of passions renders us more and more disincarnate. As we lose a felt presence in the heart, our bodies are rendered less capable of transmitting graceful presence and of receiving Eucharistic joy. It is like having been too long in front of the loudspeakers of a rock concert, we can no longer hear the crickets in the evening or appreciate the beauty of the evening light. In our growing numbness, we seek greater and greater stimulations and thrills through imagination and fall deeper into unconsciousness of the passions. Deep silence and stillness are the cure for this condition, as St. Gregory of Sinai explains,

> Nothing so fills the heart with contrition and humbles the soul as solitude embraced with self-awareness, and utter silence. And nothing so destroys the state of inner stillness and takes away the divine power that comes from it as the following six universal passions: insolence, gluttony, talkativeness, distraction, pretentiousness and the mistress of the passions, self-conceit. Whoever commits himself to these passions plunges himself progressively into darkness *until he becomes completely insensate* [emphasis added].[232]

In spite of all this, we naively imagine ourselves more spiritual and more theologically advanced than the ancient ones, largely because of our comfortable lifestyles, our identification with subjectivity and personality and by seeing human rationality as the measure of all things, whose "progress" is demonstrated by the magic wand of our increasing technological prowess. Our presumptions toward accepting theological reform based on rational rather than neptic premises makes for an illusion of spiritual progress based on human justice rather than obedience to divinely revealed Truth. Power is embraced over the constraints of conscience and privileges the seeming "freedom" of individual self-actualization over self-sacrificing obedience

---

232   Palmer, Sherrard and Ware, eds. *Philokalia* Vol IV. p. 235.

to God embraced in response to communion with the whole spiritual commonwealth.

All this is evidence of a state of collective beguilement through identification with our minds and imagination, without the sobering corrective reality that the limitations and finiteness of our bodies provide in the face of certain death. Olivier Clement suggests that for this reason, it is needful to prepare ourselves before we study the neptic Fathers. "We have to learn to pay attention to our own bodily nature—"to draw the incorporeal into the corporeal" as John Climacus says—by living the most humble sensation with gratitude, by putting with gratitude our hand on the bark of a tree, by receiving with gratitude the evening breeze on our sun-burnt skin."[233] We must do this actively, *intentionally* and apprehend directly in this way the *otherness* of Creation, every particle of which has the capacity to testify to the Creator, if only we clear the cobwebs from our hearts. There is an immense intelligence to the felt sense of the body that can only be perceived by direct awareness of the nous. This is a qualitatively distinct impression from mere sensualism or the more removed "knowing about" it in concepts, words or ratio, while lacking the intelligence of direct incarnational experience.

St. Irenaeus, a disciple of St. Polycarp, who was a disciple of St. John the Apostle who leaned on the Lord's breast, was very definite about the role of our embodied state that characterizes authentic spiritual life in Christ. In his writing *Against the Heresies,* he emphasized "Spiritual men are not incorporeal spirits; but our substance, that is the union of our flesh and spirit, receiving the Spirit of God, makes up the spiritual man."[234] Olivier Clement, in his excellent and illuminating essay on "Life in the Body"[235] describes the Patristic view of the heart that includes both mind and body and existential engagement in a way that helps modern western consciousness avoid

---

233   Ibid. Clement, Olivier, p. 138.

234   St. Irenaeus, *Against the Heresies* in The Ante-Nicene Fathers, (Roberts and Donaldson, trans.) Michigan: Eerdmans Publishing Company, 1950, p. 534.

235   Clement, Olivier, "Life in the Body," *The Ecumenical Review.* From a paper delivered at the Congress of the Fratemite Orthodoxe in Avignon, France, in November, 1980.

the old Neoplatonist and later, Descartesian dualism that frequently distorts our understanding of the neptic Fathers' approach to prayer. In his defense of the Hesychasts, St. Gregory Palamas fought against disembodied approaches to prayer in his time as well. "The practice of making the nous abandon, not the physical thoughts, but the body itself in order to come upon rational spectacles, is the strangest of the Greek delusions and the root and source of demons and the punishment which gives birth to despair and is the offspring of madness."[236] Commenting on St. Simeon the New Theologian, Fr. Staniloae points to this same understanding with respect to the noetic illumination that comes from beyond the senses. "The knowledge of God through 'seeing' comes about only through the mind being united with the body."[237] Moreover, as St. Diadochus points out, the body participates in the joy brought by the Spirit. "In those who are advancing in spiritual knowledge, grace brings an ineffable joy to their body through the perceptive faculty of the intellect."[238]

For this to make sense, it is important to understand that by "heart" the Fathers understood a depth of humanity that betrays neither body nor soul, but is faithful to the revelation of Christ who is both fully God and fully human, fully uncreated Spirit and fully created human flesh, seamlessly and unconfusedly united in one person.

> The human spirit is therefore not "something", it is this profound "heart", the innermost center where the person gathers and opens the created "flesh" to be vivified, by the breath of God. Thus the flesh becomes "spiritual". On the other hand, if a person retreats into himself or herself, the "flesh" designates the closed finitude, sealed by death, of a creature separated from God.[239]

This helps us realize that our dissociated states of "worldliness" as well as our disembodied attempts to move beyond our flesh toward

---

236   St. Gregory Palamas, *The Triads On Behalf of the Holy Hesychasts* (Ed. John Meyendorf) (trans. Nicholas Gendle) Mahwah, NJ: Paulist Press, 1983. Book 1, ii.
237   Staniloae, D. *The Experience of God, Vol II*, p. 78.
238   *The Philokalia, Volume One*, p. 281.
239   Op. Cit. p. 130.

merger with some sort of Absolute, constitute an incomplete orien-
tation to the energies of our own being-in-the-world and leads to a
spiritual and psychosocial developmental arrest of human potential
to acquire the *likeness* of God through faith and ascetical fidelity to
the divine noetic personal energies of Grace.

The Christian solution to the problem of existence is not to
remove ourselves from it, but to embrace it fully as He embraces it.
The path of prayer is not a path of withdrawing from the physical
"body" or the "sensory world" per se. That would be antihuman and
as problematic as becoming a slave to the body without obedience to
the Spirit in some kind of libertinism which St. Paul decried. St. Paul
was clear and emphatic that "We do not war against flesh and blood,
but with powers and principalities and the rulers of darkness of this
world and against spiritual wickedness in high places."[240] What is
meant by Jesus when He says "enter your closet and shut the door"[241]
in order to contend with these temptations, is a re-orientation to
embodiment itself; a deeper and more intelligent communion. It is
metanoia, the renewal of our hearts noetically through the mind that
allows us to be in the world as God intends. We are fully alive in
the flesh while at the same time enlivened by the noetic energies of
Grace, so that like the Apostles on Mt. Tabor and St. Seraphim with
Motovilov in the forest, we are able to experience the Holy Spirit's
presence which is made palpable through all five senses, a world illumined by the uncreated invisible energies of Grace and restored to
its natural state.

To help us avoid confusion it is helpful to keep in mind that in
ancient Hebrew there was no word for "body" as we have come to
view this in modern times, as distinct from "soul" or psyche in a dual-
istic way. Otherwise we tend toward a variety of wrong orientations
to our experience that fail to comprehend the potential and possi-
bilities of humankind as seen through the radical reorienting lens
of Christianity in its depth, articulated and lived by the Fathers of
the first centuries of Apostolic times and continued by the witness
of the neptic Fathers of the *Philokalia*. We are products of an overly

---

240   Eph. 16:12–13.
241   Mt. 6:6.

rationalistic, dissociated and verbally-preoccupied postmodern worldview that has emotional attachment to concepts and cultural perspectives that split "body" and "soul" or conflate them in a backwards looking neo-pagan naturalism and New Age syncretism that confuse Spirit and psyche. Each of these extreme directions fails to appreciate the uncreated dimension of the Spirit as much as a materialistic, secular rational humanism does. Each regard *human being* in ways that does not correspond to the God-given realities which are spoken about by the Fathers even though in many cases familiar Christian theological language and Scripture are being used. As Paul wrote to Timothy, these "have the form of religion but without its power."²⁴²

Without a common language rooted in shared experiential touchstones for what the neptic Fathers language refers too, as noted by St. Makarios in the quotation at the beginning of this chapter, we cannot adequately grasp what they meant by *heart*. We end up using their words and concepts wrongly, understood idiosyncratically from within our own internalized limited and distorted cultural world-views, things that lead us to a variety of dead ends like splits between reason and feelings, mind and body. Or by imagining ourselves to have already encountered and experienced the subtle realities of which they speak, whose veracity is best authenticated by a sanctified and holy life in the Image and *likeness* of Christ.

Discoveries in immunology and neurophysiology such as those of Candace Pert, former chief of brain chemistry at the National Institute of Mental Health, who first identified the neuropeptide system throughout the body as a kind of "second brain," have led some modern researchers to find it more accurate to speak of the "bodymind" based on its seamless interactive functionality, rather than as the two being separate.²⁴³ For example, endorphins (one of the body's natural opiates which is important in mood and responsible for the runners high, etc.) are produced at other sites than the brain, such as in certain white blood cells and in the gastrointestinal tract which also has receptor sites for them showing a much more organically related

---

242   2 Tim. 3:5.
243   Vid. in Candace Pert, *Molecules of Emotion: The Science Behind Mind-Body Medicine*. Simon & Schuster: New York. 1999

unity between brain and body. Dr. Pert has suggested that in terms of the complexity of this system operating beneath conscious awareness, that in some significant ways, the body *is* the unconscious.

> If we accept the idea that (neuro)peptides and other informational substances are the biochemicals of emotion, their distribution in the body's nerves has all kinds of significance. The body is the unconscious mind! Repressed traumas caused by overwhelming emotion can be stored in a body part, thereafter affecting our ability to feel that part or even move it. The new work suggests there are almost infinite pathways for the conscious mind to access—and modify—the unconscious mind and the body.[244]

These observations are congruent with the emerging understanding of trauma and how it is healed through therapies involving mind-body unity as well as with the neptic Fathers' approach to prayer which includes as its foundation, that the mind should be drawn 'inside the body' and remain alert from the heart, to thoughts as well as any proprioceptive movements in prayer, in order to remain grounded and avoid distraction. We can understand this as an ascetical effort to reunite mind and body consciously so as to approach the "natural' unity of the human being in contrast to the unnatural fragmentation[245] that characterizes our fallen condition in which the passions and imagination hold sway. Word and deed become one. St. Maximus the Confessor points out that God's wisdom is revealed in the "marvelous mixture of opposites" in which God "combined intellect and sensation through the spirit…to fashion man after His own image."[246] "The soul", he writes, "lies midway between God and

---

244 Ibid, p. 141.

245 St. Maximus the Confessor and other Fathers describe the consequences of the fall as bringing about a fragmentation of the soul in which the intellect left the heart and identified with desires, reason and imagination, becoming subject to captivity to Creation instead of fulfilling the vocation of its priesthood. Cf. Panayiotis Nellas, *Deification in Christ*. Crestwood, NY: St. Vladimir's Seminary Press, 1987.

246 Maximus the Confessor, *On the Difficulties in the Church Fathers, The Ambigua*, Vol. I. (trans. Nicholas Constas), Cambridge, MA: Harvard University Press,

matter and has faculties that unite it with both."[247] Prayer of the heart restores the soul to its natural condition of unity. Commenting on St. Maximus, Panayiotis Nellas describes this restored condition in which all the senses function as extensions of the noetically awakened heart to convey the spiritual essences of Creation which testify to the Creator's glory. The intellect must be withdrawn into the heart so that there exists a "between" that separates the soul from the "otherness" of Creation.

> Thus not only can the soul, if it uses the senses correctly, "through its own proper faculties" organize and govern the world, while at the same time keeping the world external to itself, but, and this is fundamental, it also has the power to convey "wisely to itself everything visible in which God is concealed and proclaimed in silence."[248]

This restored condition of the heart is in contrast to the monological incorporation of Creation that characterizes the fall in which the soul is held captive by the objectification of Creation as it attempts, without divine blessing, to grasp what is desired, and so becomes a slave to an autoerotic process driven by addiction to pleasure rather than a dialogical one which is supported by ascetical fidelity and characterized by Eucharistic joy.

At the beginning stages of prayer, loss of awareness of our body, usually via imagination and day-dreaming, is a distraction, a form of inattentiveness and dissociation, forgetfulness of the life that we *are,* a life that is meant to be transfigured with the divine energies. With patience and perseverance, ascetical struggle with our attention inwardly, motivated by faith and love, eventually leads to infusion with the divine energies of Grace that prove transformative to the whole person, body included. In the higher stages of noetic prayer, under the influence of the Holy Spirit in this way, as St. Paul and numerous others since have confirmed, while one is for a time, in a

---

2014, p. 3.
  247 Maximus the Confessor, *Ambigua,* PG 91, 1097C.
  248 Panayiotis Nellas, Deification in Christ. Crestwood, NY: St. Vladimir's Seminary Press, 1987, p. 55.

very different way, no longer aware of body or even of the ordinary rational mind, the body nevertheless remains present. "I know that this man, whether in the body or not I do not know, but God knows, was caught up to Paradise and heard inexpressible things, things that no one is permitted to tell."[249] St. Isaac the Syrian describes this degree and type of noetic illumination under the influence of the divine energies as qualitatively different than seeking insight through ordinary mental processes or ascetical struggle. He refers to this kind of revelation as "motionlessness of the mind" and states clearly that it is altogether beyond the senses and rationality in its origins and apprehension. "A man does not by human diligence and reflection devise some image for the discovery of knowledge, but it comes by a spiritual working, when he to whom the revelation is given is at that moment aware neither of any thought in his soul, nor of any of those things before his sense, nor does he have anything to do with them or even know of them."[250]

Preparation for prayer involves ascetical struggle inwardly to collect ourselves and from a mind-body-unified presence, seeking to call on the Lord from the place of the heart, which is a still deeper inward organ that is one with our human life and capable of noetically receiving the uncreated divine energies of Grace. Recognizing our experiential and linguistic distance from the Fathers makes it even more critical that we seek to re-member ourselves in stillness, silence, and with a collected presence, in order to approach the writings of the holy Fathers on the basis of experiential touchstones in a way that we can begin to benefit from their experience by confirming it for ourselves. It is necessary that we embark experientially on the path of prayer and repentance to discover the "hidden person of the heart"[251] by the power of the Holy Spirit who responds to Christ who is seeking us. This is evidenced by the intensity of our

---

249 2 Cor. 12:13–14.

250 "On the different kinds of revelations and [divine] workings given to saints in images and likeness, Appendix A. *The Ascetical Homilies of St. Isaac the Syrian.* Revised second edition. Trans. From the Greek and Syriac, Holy Transfiguration Monastery, Boston, MA, 2011, p. 540.

251 1 Pet. 3:4.

seeking the Father in return, "Abba, Father!"[252] such that St. Gregory of Nyssa points to the paradox of the endless fervent search for the One who cannot be contained: "Who seeks God endlessly has found Him."[253]

This is why it is good to remind ourselves that faith, hope and love for Christ are much more than technical means. According to St. John of the Ladder, "God appears to the mind in the heart, at first as a flame purifying its lover, and then as a light which illumines the mind and renders it God-like."[254] This reminds us that above all, prayer is *personal.* God is our true lover and "He pursues, without fail and at all costs, the sighs of our hearts, which mean far more than any obligatory or formal asceticism. The spiritual life depends significantly on the character of these sighs,"[255] for they are the recognition that we are human, a fact we only truly experience in the process of acquiring a "crushed and humbled heart"[256]

If in response to divine love, attention that is directed by our will arising from deep within the *heart of flesh*[257] meets resistance from the denying force of the fallen dissociated *heart of stone*, which as St. James points out, is preoccupied with the temptations arising from thoughts that tempt us toward sin and egoistic worldliness, then the deciding factor or transformative catalyst in this spiritual battle of "double-mindedness unstable in all our ways"[258] is the Holy Spirit—the Divine energies of Grace acting on our heart through our consent. This "noetic intercourse"[259] offers humanity a chance to overcome the deterministic inertia of polarities; our slavery to pleasure and pain, like and dislike, that stand guard at the door disrupting

---

252 Gal. 4:6.

253 Cited in Cardenal, E. *Abide in Love*, New York: Orbis Books, 1955, p. 64.

254 Cited by Nicephorus the Solitary, *Writings from the Philokalia*, London: Faber & Faber, 1975, p. 24.

255 Archimandrite Arsenios (Papacioc), "Eternity Hidden in the Moment," *The Orthodox Word*. No. 281 (2011), p. 289.

256 Psalm 51:17.

257 Ezek. 36:26.

258 James 1:6.

259 "Prayer may be defined as the intellect's unceasing intercourse with God." St. Niketas Stethatos, Philokalia Vol. IV. p. 129.

stillness and the path to prayer of the heart that arises from ascetical fidelity in response to love for Christ.

Repentance arises as the contradictions and difficulties we experience reveal our helplessness and convinces us of our need for God to help us so that we can cry out from the heart in prayer. This action of remaining attentive to the struggle between the energies of affirmation (intention) and denial (distraction, inclinations toward sin) is the ascetical effort analogous to the "steward of the inner household"[260] that anticipates and prepares for the arrival of the Master. This standing and waiting on Christ in the midst of these resistances is itself relational and more "me" than the string of identifications with imagination and various thoughts and automatic associations that happen throughout the day which I generally take as "myself." Evagrius counsels, "If you wish to know who you are, do not look at what you have been, but at what you were originally created."[261]

The spiritual beguilement of daily life is a kind of running monologue that is a function of my lack of attention and inner collected watchfulness. In actuality, the string of "self" reflections are constitutive of my inner press-secretary's ever expanding portfolio of self-glorification, attempts to define myself on my own. Even the sum of these pictures do not constitute "me" but represent only the collection of fragmented inner states more or less distorted by the passions, each vying for the place of my true life which is "hid with Christ in God"[262] and only comes into being through *dia-Logos*, free of passions in synergy with God's Grace in relation to all others and in such a way that the 'left hand doesn't know what the right hand is doing." In other words, my ordinary "I" can never really know or accurately evaluate "myself" as an "object" apart from being-in-relationship with God and in relationship with others whom God loves, because I receive my true being only in and through relationship with God and the Creation. "God alone, who is love, can *know* me and so repentance and love, both relational events, become the more

260 Lk. 12:42.
261 Kadloubovsky, E. and Palmer, G.E.H. (eds.) *Early Fathers from the Philokalia*. Faber and Faber Limited: London, 1976, p. 109.
262 Col. 3:13.

accurate experience of the self-in-relationship with God and others. Repentance is a response to communion and opens the way to love. Fr. Staniloae captures this succinctly when he writes, "For myself, in so far as I am not loved, I am incomprehensible."[263]

From this perspective, I begin to realize that in my fallen state I am continuously using the Lord's holy Name, "I AM," *in vain*. From a fragmented inner state, divided by passions, my lips speak but my body and mind are not united and my words do not proceed from my heart. This is akin to what St. Silouan pointed out to Fr. Stratonicos when he revealed a mystery of the Spirit to him which the latter had not yet fully grasped. "The perfect never say anything of themselves… They only say what the Spirit inspires them to say."[264] Jesus Christ alone is perfect speech, for as He said, the Son of God does nothing by himself, but only what He sees the Father doing. "Whatever the Father does, the Son also does."[265] For a human being to approach this of course presumes a state of continuous repentance, of freedom from identification with all those thoughts capturing my weak attention that only serve my *kenodoxia* (vainglory). St. Silouan, by contrast, points to the fruits of a Grace-filled state of continuous prayer and remembrance of God. My actual condition is far from this. I hear the words but I cannot live them. I cannot *do* what I *say*. To paraphrase St. Paul, "The noetic prayer I would pray, I do not, and the beguilement I would not enter into, that I lose myself in, weak-willed, poorly attentive and inexperienced man that I am. Who can save me from this dying see-saw of polarity between love for Christ and idolatrous preoccupation with my vainglorious self? Thanks be to Christ Who *is* Truth and the gateway into the Holy Trinity!"[266] He is the "Way" that leads to everlasting life involving my 'intention' and 'attention' to continuous repentance repeated over and

---

263 Staniloae, D. *The Experience of God: Orthodox Dogmatic Theology, Vol. I. The Experience of God*, Brookline, MA: Holy Cross Orthodox Press, 1998, p. 25.

264 Sophrony. A. St. *Silouan the Athonite*. Essex, England: St. John the Baptist Stavropegic Monastery, 1999. p. 57.

265 Jn. 5:19.

266 cf. Rom. 7:19, 7:24–25.

over daily throughout a lifetime in response to growing love for Him and for the creation He loves.

A simple experiment shows the difficulty of watchfulness and prayer. Try attending to reading of the Holy Gospels or the Divine Liturgy with presence, without allowing any intervening thoughts between the words and the apprehension of the heart in a state of collected, embodied attention as though you were looking into the eyes of your beloved. The first moment you become aware of wandering thoughts that intervene, re-collect yourself and begin again. See how many times in the space of 5 minutes, presence is dispersed as the attention is caught up with something other than the felt sense and meaning of the words.

As a young seminarian with great expectations and illusions about myself, I was given a simple challenge not to touch my face over the course of an hour-long bus ride. I failed. Later the question was asked, "If you can't even restrain yourself from touching your face for one hour, what makes you think you are able to obey the commandments of Jesus Christ?" What a wonderful introduction to an idealistically imagined and hoped-for prayerful attention, stillness, and watchfulness in daily life. Repeated experiences of being humbled by catching glimpses of my *actual* choices, thoughts and reactivity in daily life as distinct from my idealized picture of myself, begins to fuel a real cry to God for help. It becomes obvious that I need divine help in response to my meagre efforts, to be attentive in prayer. So often in daily life we do not pay sufficient attention to our thoughts or how the movement of our bodies and tones of voice express our inner state of identification with thoughts and imagination and we become dominated by resulting passions. This does not mean analyzing ourselves, but a direct perception of *what is*. We are constantly identified with all these inner movements in the moment without realizing the necessity for continuing struggle between the automaticity of our habits and the desire for a greater response-ability to Truth and Love that grows in proportion to the prayer and watchfulness that are born out of that struggle.

This is even more difficult in situations and with people we have become accustomed to. I hear the familiar words of Scripture and my attention wanders in response to the automatic presumption that "I've heard this before. I already know what it means." The words are so familiar, in spite of the deacon's reminders in the Divine Liturgy "Let us attend!" My response is mechanical instead of from a receptive heart where these words can have a certain action they do not otherwise have. In this regard, the saying is true, "Whoever has [attention in the heart] to him more shall be given, and he will have in abundance, but whoever does not have, even what he has shall be taken away from him."[267]

A very high quality of intentional, repeatedly renewed, inner attention in the present moment is necessary in order to be present in a fresh way to what I have heard many times before so that deeper meanings are revealed. This kind of attention arises out of love and the recognition born of repentance, that our *real* life lies in the experience of vulnerability and dialogical reciprocity with "the One Who is" in the Eternal Now, and not as a function of self-initiated "strategic planning" and "time management." The tendency to constantly need new stimulation "from the outside" to overcome my inability to keep noetically awake inwardly in the face of the familiar, is a large part of the human problem. Repeated observations reveal that my mind tends to stay on the surface of experience living in the past (or the future) and easily growing bored. God lives in the eternal present hidden behind experience and cannot be encountered as something already known or as a stimulating new imagined object, but only Eucharistically, relationally, through faith.

How then do we respond to the injunction to attend and to seek "continuous prayer and repentance" in daily life so that this Eucharistic reciprocity actually becomes an active questioning of myself, a sustained "unknowing" interest in the One who is beyond my senses and rationality *here* and *now*? How can I discover from moment to moment what prevents me, like the rich young ruler,[268] from *letting go* of what I have collected, especially the constituents of what seems to be my "self" in order to encounter Christ in communion with and through the world and people around me? "For whoever seeks to

---

267 Mt. 13:12; (Mk. 4:25; Lk. 19:26.)
268 Vid. Lk. 18:18–27.

save his life will lose it but whoever loses [the vainglorious self] for the sake of life in Me, will save his life."[269] Can I begin to see that the "Way" to life and to love, begins at a *deeper level of embodiment* than word associations whose center of gravity remain in imaginings "up in my head" or merely ideologically grasped by emotional zeal as a means of preserving a subtle and illusory sense of superiority compared to others?

Can I discover prayer that is more than hedonistically collecting emotional experiences I find soothing and self-calming? Can I begin to realize prayer is impossible apart from encounter with God in the present moment involving repentance which is always beyond my control? As Archimandrite Meletios Webber points out, this makes for a struggle because

> the mind cannot trust the present moment, since it cannot control it, and is thus almost always at enmity with it… The mind cannot control the present moment, the time during which things can arise, so it pretends that it does not exist. This causes a person to behave in a completely unconscious way, forcing the individual to wait for the mind to absorb an event (which by then has become an event in the past) before she or he is allowed to experience it.[270]

Prayer is only fulfilled in personal relationship with the incorporeal God in and through the God-Man Jesus Christ in the eternal now. It is fundamentally dialogical and not monological. The Church is a relational context of love and not a matter of private "self-actualization." As it has been said, "We are saved together but we fall alone."

Prayer is intimacy and vulnerability that involve surrender of all acquisitions of the man-made self that render us in any way "better than" our fellows or preserve a sense of entitlement based on our own achievements. Without the Holy Spirit's initiation from beyond the

---

269   Mt. 16:25; Lk 9:24.
270   Archimandrite Meletios Webber, *Bread & Water, Wine & Oil* Indiana: Conciliar Press, 2007.

created order, prayer is ineffectual and love unrequited, regardless of the quality of collected human attention and the ascetical efforts made. Archimandrite Sophrony has spoken very clearly regarding this distinction, dogmatically and experientially, in his discussion of how Hindu and Buddhist forms of ascetical and meditative practice differ from Orthodox Christian prayer[271] in that meditation, per se, is not dialogical and can involve states of spiritual beguilement at advanced levels of refined consciousness which, however blissful, fail to reach the uncreated personal hypostases of the Holy Trinity. He writes:

> All other paths deflect our mind from the personal interrelationship between God and the one who prays into the realm of an abstract trans-personal Absolute, into impersonal asceticism. In diverting our mind from all images, meditation can afford us a sense of tranquility, of peace, of release from time and space, but there is no feeling of standing before a personal God. It is not real prayer—face to Face. This can lead to a state where one who is entranced by meditation will be content with the psychical results of such experiments and, worst of all, perception of the Living God, the Personal Absolute, will be alien to him.[272]

So, from the beginning, we strive to withdraw our attention away from its zig-zagging flights of identification with discursive thoughts, projection of fantasies, and visions, all of which disperse mind-body unity and draw our attention and imagination, "out" through the senses or the imagination, as it were, objectifying the world in a monological embrace. This was Barlaam's mistake, and arguably that of the whole scientific revolution,[273] thinking that reason could know

---

271 Vid. Sophrony, Archimandrite, *We Shall See Him As He Is*. Essex, England: Stavropegic Monastery of St. John the Baptist, 1988.

272 Sophrony, A. *On Prayer*, Crestwood, NY: St. Vladimir's Seminary Press, 1996, p. 139.

273 For a cogent and clear examination of this thesis, see Sherrard, P. *The Eclipse of Man and Nature: An Enquiry into the Origins and Consequences of Modern Science.* Vermont: Inner Traditions/Lindisfarne Press, 1987.

God or one's own self as an object, merely conceptually or by systematic examination of the projective process. This is a seedbed for unde-
tected pride, as though humanity could stand outside ourselves and
Creation and come to know realty in this way apart from undergoing
the mystery of Communion with the One who is beyond the created
order. The knowing of oneself through repentance that St. Isaac the
Syrian praises "is greater than one who raises the dead"[274] is based
on encountering and being encountered by Christ, through the Holy
Spirit, and one another as 'other', not by monologically incorporating
the other or totalizing and objectifying the other as though my own
subjective experience fully captured the essence of the other. There is
no love in this monological kind of "knowing", no dia-Logos, which
is arises "Wherever *two or more* gather in my name, I AM in their
midst."[275]

In the final analysis, if we want to encounter God it is because
God has already sought us out and we are responding to this. "It is
not that we love God but that God first loved us"[276] as St. John the
Theologian points out, that is always the starting point. Responding
to God's call, it is necessary to keep lassoing the attention from its
wanderings to "other gods", other objects of attention. This happens
constantly until compunction arises in response to Grace. Whenever you become aware that your unruly attention has wandered,
re-establish awareness of the mind-body presence and from the place
of the heart, turn to Christ either in silent intent or in the words of
the prayer. Be sure this watchfulness and "guarding the heart" occur
within a real proprioceptive sense of bodily presence and not merely
in the disembodied "imagination" while unaware of the body. Psychic
fantasy of prayer is not the same thing as intentionally praying with
attention collected in the heart with the attention drawn out of the
imagination and within the physical body. One of the letters to a
spiritual child on this subject records a conversation between Elder
Haralambos of Mt. Athos, an experienced ascetical struggler and

274 *The Ascetical Homilies of Saint Isaac the Syrian,* Revised Second Edition,
Holy Transfiguration Monastery, Boston, 2011, p. 461.
275 Mt. 18:20.
276 I Jn. 4:10.

teacher of noetic prayer, and a Greek Orthodox visitor who wanted to speak with the elder about noetic prayer.

—Father, I am a mystic like you.

—Mysticism? Where did you learn that?

—I have been in Germany for years now. I came to know other religions there. They have many things that are similar to us. That which I liked a lot is that they meditate on prayer. And the most significant is that they come to a state of ecstasy and contemplation, like St. Paul did.

—Hey, keep your distance. Don't believe that. They are deluded.

—No, Father. I have also got involved and have experienced it myself.

—(Not that I was convinced, but out of curiosity), I asked: Why, tell me. What meditation is it that you do?

—I sit down with my legs crossed and turn my head to heaven. Through this, I have understood that everyone in the world believe in the same God. The Hindus pray to their God, the Buddhists do the same. We can pray to Christ.

—And, if I may ask, how do you pray?

—Ah, here is the secret, which you don't know. You imagine with your mind that you are flying to the heavens; that you are seeing angels fly; you are seeing gold palaces, lights, brightness, and so on, and in the end you are seeing Christ, in bright light, sitting on a fiery throne. We concentrate with all our attention on that which we are imagining.

—Hey, deluded one. With these things, you are going to lose your mind as well. Is that how they pray?

—Well, wait and you will marvel, and then you can criticize. Since we force our imagination as much as we can, suddenly we leave this sphere. Then all that we have been imaging, we see. Do you know what it is to see

Christ, to see the angels, the saints, and many wondrous things?

—Do you want to hear me, my child? Give these things up, so that you don't lose your mind as well. We close all the doors to fantasy to find Christ inside us. With fantasy, you open all of Satan's doors. Do you read the holy Bible? Do you believe that the devil has the power to appear like an angel of light, even like Christ Himself?

—But don't you believe? I told you, we see Christ with our eyes, not in our sleep. I even saw Buddha, once. He is great, but not like Christ.

—My child, it's a pity Satan is fooling you. You are going to lose your faith as well.

—No, no, Father. I don't believe you. We don't agree.

—(He left and he was still saying to himself,) "No, I don't agree. God is not the monopoly of monks" and other such things. Do you hear, my child, how many delusions there are, how many dangers there are?[277]

Sub-vocalizing words "in the head," or with the lips, while not having a connection with a unified body and mind is mechanical and routine and open to delusion. In the same way, thinking about having a body or imagining having a body are not the same as actually being *present as body*. The embodied state is an antidote to imagination and the heart is the deeper place within the embodied presence, from which sensation, feelings and thoughts can be observed. All that is noetically encountered, is communicated to the body and feelings. The heart is the connecting point between mind and body that is "warmed" and illumined by the noetic infusion of Grace. When the words are "prayed" it is because they come from the heart. By contrast, in the distracted state, the mind "wanders" away from the body as imagination subtly intercedes between the mind outside of the heart. Or lacking watchfulness, the attention dissolves by merging

277 Monk Joseph. *Abbot Haralambos Dionysiatis, The Teacher of Noetic Prayer,* Athens, Greece: H. Monastery Dionysiou, pp. 207- 208

into the sensation of the body as sensuality or into dreams as sleepiness. Either way, the deeper inner attention of the nous is being captured even while the superficial mind is sub-vocalizing the words of the prayer. To avoid this, some fathers suggest returning to spoken prayer to attract the attention back into the body and away from fantasy by allowing the ear to hear the words spoken. But it is also possible, when we notice this fall into inattention in prayer, to return to the fully embodied state and place our attention on the meaning and intention of the words of the prayer from within heart. We repeatedly force this gently until the moment arises when the heart takes up the words itself.

This same struggle is true in prayer whether eyes are open or closed. The mind constantly becomes occupied with various illusions seeking to fill in the empty bare presence whenever there is the slightest inattention. Neptic wakefulness, intentional stillness and yearning in the heart are all active states in prayer and must be constantly renewed. The hesychastic method of prayer refers to this active intentional journey inward toward a "union of the mind in the heart in prayer, such that the whole of man (with all the faculties of his soul and body) prays purely and becomes wholly pure prayer."[278]

When you are set to begin prayer, be sure that physical stillness and inner concentration are united. There may be some initial struggle with *logismoi* in the form of prepossessions, memories of old sins, or the surfacing of certain attitudes and beliefs or that interfere with stillness; a sense of "being alone" and "talking to the air" or "I've done this before and it doesn't work" or "it would be more profitable to read spiritual books than sit here doing nothing," etc., etc., may occur. All kinds of resistances spring up when there is a desire to be still and neptically alert in order to truly pray. If you recognize this and persist in "sinking below the waves" of the dispersed mind, toward the place of the heart, persisting in your intention to pray and hoping in God's help, a change will eventually occur. From this collected foundation of mind-body unity, allow your attention to "draw in" the Jesus prayer

278 Jean-Claude Larchet, *Therapy of Spiritual Illnesses: An Introduction to the Ascetic Tradition of the Orthodox Church, Vol. I- III*. Montreal, Canada: Alexander Press, 2012, p. 249.

with your breathing. Or perhaps better said, let it "be drawn in" naturally, by loving attention to Christ in faith—not by attachment to any image or by attempting to make anything happen—but simply as bare attention and grateful awareness of the *thatness* of being present before Christ in this way and cognizant of the certainty of our creaturely death.

Gradually the presence deepens and a kind of "interest" or "thirst" develops for the imageless, movementless presence of Christ Who is already in our hearts knocking at the door waiting for us to answer. There may be a sense of recognition that presence is related to the anticipated encounter with Christ who has no form and no physical substance and cannot be penetrated by the effort of any kind of human knowing, but who has already come to us and assumed us already in Him. Trusting this, let God teach the rest according to His timing. **All we can really expect ourselves to do is to "show up" as best we are able for the anticipated and longed-for meeting. The rest is for God to accomplish in and through us.**[279] Maybe we can only show up "a little," but as in the story of the Prodigal,[280] once the Father is watching for us and when He sees us turning ever so slightly toward home, he runs to meet us the entire rest of the way.

This active "intention" and higher quality of "attention" reveals to God our disposition and gives wings to our wish for God. At the time of prayer it is our offering to God—our five loaves and two fish[281] that we bring to Christ. This is the only aspect of ourselves at the moment that we can manage to bring forward to Him. We have no virtues. He is virtue. We have only sins. We have no life. He is life. And then we wait for Christ to offer us to God for a blessing and receive us back, blessed and changed, like the anaphora that becomes a liturgy of love. As often as we can, we renew this effort, re-membering ourselves in this way, each time we realize we have forgotten, with our focus on Christ Who is invisibly present. In this way, we are offering our ascetical labor to "show up" with our

---

279   In the simplest sense, it might have been better to say only this and leave aside the rest...

280   Vid. Lk. 15:20.

281   Vid. Mt. 14:17.

body, mind, soul and strength. When we try this regularly, as a prayer rule, we become aware of how weak our zeal is and how fragile and unstable is our capacity to remain "awake" like this in the hour of the Lord's Gethsemane prayer for us. He is present to our human condition fully, at all times and in all places, awake to both the terror, the wounds and helpless loss of everything that ends in death, which we cannot escape. And He is present in the utter mystery and unutterable joy of the fact that we have been called into being out of nothing through Him as a manifestation of the Logos, as beings who can contribute our own free choice to receive from him the power to be in his *likeness* as well. What is our response-ability for this gift of life that we are? Prayer begins to reveal this to us.

At some point in a way we don't know how, and at a time we cannot predict, prayer that has been drawn down from "up in the head," to a locus "beneath" the wandering thoughts or sub-vocalizations begins to be taken up by the heart. There is a subtle "felt" sense that has a different "taste" than ordinary physical sensation or mental imagining alone or even "feelings." One begins to feel a mild "thirst" for prayer that cascades and bubbles effortlessly like a small stream from the heart. This arises from the direction or location of the "hidden person of the heart" which we begin to discover at this threshold. The center of gravity shifts from our effortful egoistic "doing" to a kind of responsive full-personed entering into and receiving prayer. It is from this deeper place of the heart where our conscience resides that tears arise. The presence becomes palpable and relational and the words and intention of prayer being expressed become more of a "deed" that comes from one's heart, rather than merely words of the lips or sub-vocalizations of the ego-driven will of the mind and body. This is also the place where confession begins, when the nous enters the heart. One prays...and yet one is prayed simultaneously.

Tears of compunction arise in response to the invisible hope in the presence of God known in faith. There is no need to do anything but respond to the movement of the heart turning now toward Christ in joyful sorrow, hope, gratefulness and love. This movement may not actually express itself in words, but only intention. Tears may come even more forcefully with the intention or bring forth words and sighs that are being "prayed" from the heart, inspired, rather than forced by our will or sub-vocalizations, etc. This is accompanied by a distinct change, which you will know by its taste when it occurs. But don't try to step outside it and objectify it, or the encounter will be lost. Let Grace do its work in you simply without interfering. Elder Ephraim of Katounakia says

> With the Jesus prayer come tears. Tears are somewhere between passion and dispassion; tears purify. There are beginner's tears, meaning the tears which come when you wonder: "What if I fall into sin? Will I be with Christ or the devil? What if I am in hell eternally?" Thoughts like that. Then come the tears of Grace. These tears are so sweet that every time I shed them I used say: "Dear God, when I am in Paradise I want nothing else but to cry tears like these." These tears come later on. Tears are the food of the soul. Just as the body is revitalized when fed with good food, in the same way the soul is invigorated when it is fed with tears. When you shed tears during prayer, whatever kind of tears, you move ahead. When the tears stop, you go backwards.[282]

This encounter with Grace in the heart, as distinct from "knowing about" or "observing" monologically like a scientist from the mind removed from the heart, involves a different quality of presence and relationship—both a witnessing of what is being expressed and experienced as "your own" words and longing, yet at the same time as being also something that is 'given to you" for which you are deeply grateful and which without the help of the Holy Spirit in the deeper collected presence, you could not feel or know or utter in this way on your own. This is confirmation of the presence of the otherness of God that is also closer to us than our own breath and more dear to us than our own life is known by its taste.

But *all* these things may be misleading if you attempt in any way with the imagination to "follow instructions with the head" or to

---

282   Ephraim, E. pp. 256–257.

copy something, or to try to make something happen emotionally, etc. that fits some kind of imagination you have about what "should" or "needs" to happen. These descriptions are only verbal descriptions or approximations of *something you must discover for yourself* and through this according to your humility, the Holy Spirit will show you the way forward and give you exactly what is beneficial for you in the right amount and in the proper time. In learning to acquire a taste for the goodness of God, we follow the "crumbs from the Master's table"[283] like Hansel and Gretel in the Grimm's Brothers' fairy tale, who tried to find their way out of the forest by the trail of breadcrumbs.[284] All our prayer life is a journey out of the forest of the fallen world to Christ and the Beloved Community in the Paradise of the Eucharist. He unites in His person the created and uncreated worlds, the bodiless divine essence of God and the created human body of the person with all other human persons in Christ.

Presence in prayer is palpable and the refreshment and compunction that sometimes arises, shows the direction forward. The fruits will confirm it—greater attentiveness to the soul's movements afterward, more desire for Jesus prayer, more gratefulness, more desire for obedience, and by increased thirst for reading Holy Scripture, the writers in the *Philokalia* and the saints whose words and neptic observations have occurred during deep collected presence and illumination by Grace. Most of all the litmus test of authenticity is a growing mercy and compassion toward one's fellows and humility arising from greater sensitivity to the presence of one's own egotism and sinful inclinations revealed in God's invisible light.

As we begin to experience this mystery of encounter with Grace in prayer we begin to glimpse ever so slightly that we do not want to receive the rest of our life "unworthily" without recognizing Christ in our midst and ourselves in Christ on a daily basis. He is saying to us every moment of our lives, "I am yours do with Me whatever you want." And as we mature, we begin to realize that our greatest joy is to respond to him with the same love, "I am yours do with

---

283 The Eucharistic encounter.

284 Unfortunately, in the Grimm's Brothers tale, the birds ate the crumbs, (as in the Parable of the sower, Mt. 13ff) and the children became lost in the forest.

me whatever you want." This is our living *anaphora*. But we cannot withstand the full intensity of this as He does. We are not yet mature.

We discover in our seemingly unsuccessful attempts to pray and to love, that like the Apostles, we go to sleep again and again when He invites us to stay neptically awake with Him. Realizing our true condition, shed for a moment from our illusions, we begin to cry out with more strength for help. We realize how pitiful are our puny love and care for others. We realize how little we really "exist;" how much we take for granted and judge God by our own human condition. This helps us to break out of the insulating illusions so well and memorably described by Clement of Alexandria. "Most people are enclosed in their mortal bodies like a snail in its shell, curled up in their obsessions after the manner of hedgehogs. They form their notion of God's blessedness taking themselves as a model."[285] This is the threshold of beginning to taste and see that HE IS God and we are not. The struggle calls us toward Him by responding to His love with our total self-offering. Deeper repentance is born from this dawning realization of our insignificance apart from Christ and it is humility which makes room for His presence in our hearts.

As He comes near to us we want to follow Him, but we don't know how. We are deaf, dumb, blind and paralyzed and have not realized this. In the stillness of prayer, we cry out from the heart like blind Bartimaeus.[286] We neptically climb the tree of attention as high as we can like Zacchaeus[287] and discover that the Lord is calling us to "come down" to the ground where He will meet us in our ordinary perishable human selves without any illusions or imagination of blessedness. From here He will invite us to the Eucharistic banquet of mercy where we are transformed and our fragmented nature healed. This is the unmerited Eucharistic encounter of love. We do this one thing we *can* do, over and over, like a child learning to take its first steps on wobbly legs, falling countless times, calling our attention back into our body, away from its dallying with fantasy.

---

285   Cited in Clement, O. *The Roots of Christian Mysticism: Texts From the Patristic Era With Commentary,* New City Press: New York, 1993. p. 26.

286   Vid. Mk. 10:46.

287   Vid. Lk. 19:2.

This reveals our real need and limitations over and over again. We seek as best we can to re-member ourselves and hope in the promise of the Holy Spirit to re-member us. This divine initiative we cannot control, but we hope in. It is love freely given in its own time and way. We can only pray "It is good for me to cling to God" in the stillness and darkness of bare presence, "and place in Christ the hope of my salvation."[288] We cannot lift ourselves to Christ, but He has come down from heaven to us where He dwelled among us in the flesh and gave us His own flesh and blood to drink. In His Body, Christ transforms all of creation into a Divine Liturgy, a wedding feast to which all are invited and in which, as Olivier Clement says:

> The body is called to become a liturgical body by inte-riorizing the celebration. The fundamental purpose of Orthodox ascesis and spirituality is to become aware of this rising body, sown by baptism inside the body and nourished by the Eucharist. For in its structure and its rhythms the human body is constituted to become "the temple of the Holy Spirit" as Paul says. This involves the two fundamental rhythms of respiration and of blood; and also the "space of the heart," a "space" which is both corporeal and spiritual.[289]

In prayer He invisibly calls to us to take a few steps forward to meet him Eucharistically again and again. "Behold I stand at the door and knock."[290] He says to us. "Come out and find pasture."[291] We take this step and then another, wondering how it is possible. The Holy Spirit draws us. And we face temptation with each step, like Peter walking on the water, asking inevitable, inane and presumptive questions such as "How am I doing this? How is it happening?" And the moment the eye of the *nous* in our heart takes its focus off Christ, and our attention wanders back to our own illusory control, our scientific presumption of prediction and control, we begin to sink. Like

---

288   Anonymous prayer from the Prayers Before Communion.
289   Olivier Clement, "Life in the Body" p. 135.
290   Rev. 3:20.
291   cf. Jn. 10:9.

the soul in the Song of Solomon, when the Beloved is at the door, we realize that our wandering attention is a momentary hesitation. We cry out "Lord save me I am sinking." Perhaps He does and we continue in prayer, going a little deeper into the mystery of the noetic embrace. Or if not, again out of mercy to help strengthen us, we are forced to wander barefoot through the city in search of Him Whom we lost because we "hesitated" revealing something lacking in our disposition. This too is His love, teaching us, helping us to trust him in His presence and in His absence and to discover the ways we err.

Hesitation is a sign that our heart is not yet sufficiently hungry and thirsty only for Christ. And that we are weak and immature. So, He departs and lets us rest and grow hungry again and then He returns. But each time we don't know how long we will have to wait. And while we wait, many temptations invite us to abandon the effort in favor of the easy pleasant stimulation offered by objects for our attention to involve us with that offer to give a solace that seems to be eluding us. In our unruly desire, we can easily go whoring after other gods in His absence.[292] I have heard it said, "remembrance of death is the mother of prayer." Monastic wisdom points to remembering our mortality as a means toward spiritual sobriety that invites contrition and nourishes prayer.[293] So even in the absence of presence and the pain of our helplessness to remain awake, we can wait on the Lord in the presence of our eventual certain death. It is too much for my mind and my heart…so I retreat and say "Lord Jesus Christ, Son of God, have mercy on me, the sinner" if only with my lips.

Even a half hour of stillness and watchfulness is often too much for me. Often prayer is just bearing 30 minutes of distraction without consolation and not giving up. I believe Christ, knowing our intentions, may value our persistence in this desert time even more than if we have consolations that make it easy. So we don't despair.

292 Vid. Judges 2:17.

293 St. John Climacus contrasts remembrance of death that is spiritual and evokes inner compunction with a morbid terror of death that is indicative of faithlessness and unrepented sins: "To be reminded of death each day is to die each day; to remember one's departure from life is to provoke tears by the hour. Fear of death is a property of nature due to disobedience, but terror of death is a sign of unrepented sins." From *The Ladder of Divine Ascent,* chapter 6, "On Remembrance of Death."

Prayer is the re-collecting from the heart of my whole self so that as the Psalmist says, "My soul thirsts for you. O how my flesh yearns for You!"[294] Finding the place of the heart requires the harmonious working of all the human powers. "For the Christian the main problem will be to 'lower' his clear conscience and his intelligence 'into his heart' and at the same time to transfigure the force (*thymos*) and the desire (*epithymia*) in the crucible of this reconstituted 'heart-spirit'."[295] We need not be in a cave in the desert to enter the heart. This takes places wherever compunction arises. Any occasion of the Spirit penetrating the heart and bringing tears is a small moment of noetic prayer. A gift. A taste. We are always at the threshold of encountering Christ with the opportunity to pray wherever we are. As the Orthodox prayer to the Holy Spirit suggests, "O Comforter, Spirit of Truth Who are in all places and fills all things…" What is essential is that we remember, or perhaps more accurately said, when we "are re-membered" by the Holy Spirit tapping on our hearts in the still small invisible voice with an invitation that awakens and revives the flesh, that we respond immediately. For an instant, we have a chance to make a renewed effort with gratefulness. We are inspired to 'begin again' for we do not ever "arrive" as though we could stand on our own in the House of God without breathing in God over and over and in our mortality, breathing out a wish for mercy, acquiring a fresh recognition of our dependency on Christ for our life as clearly as our next breath.

We live for the Bread of Life which is dia-Logos with God. Our I AM is the moon to God's sun which illumines us and lets us shine too. But we must learn not to ever make the tragic mistake of thinking the light shining from us originates from us! Or that my efforts are what made my prayer "successful" or that when I don't feel consolation I am a failure. This kind of vainglorious monologue born of identification with various fluctuating inner states creates all kinds of unsolvable problems as a result, including a trajectory to beguilement and ultimately despair.

---

294 Psalm 63:1.
295 Olivier Clement, "Life in the Body", p. 136.

In my easy, flabby, inattentive taking-for-grantedness of the world, and the Liturgy, prayer and others around me while eating dinner, working, interacting with the teller at the bank or playing with my grandchildren, things take place on the level of automatic mindless emotional reactivity. This is related to what St. Mark the Ascetic called the three giants of "ignorance, laziness and forgetfulness" that attempt to block our path to prayer. Through struggle and repeated glimpses of failure, I am gradually given to realize the depth and extent to which in my complacency I take life for granted moment to moment on a daily basis.

But Christianity is the path of redemption that leads to being in the world in a deeper incarnational way because we ourselves are no longer settling for identifying with pictures of ourselves, and seeking to preserve these illusions, but desiring first and foremost, an encounter with God through everyone and everything we come in contact with. This involves a deeper mindful embodied presence from which arises a greater respect for every moment; gratefulness for the gift of life. More than that, we come to realize with the Psalmist, "Your mercy is greater than life itself."[296] This is the dawning joy of a Eucharistic life, a taste of the eternal Kingdom of God wherein all these other things become what God intends them to be; bearers of His presence. This Kingdom is a path of *dia-Logos* that moves from swings of polarity that do not truly grow beyond the material, to a Trinitarian life through the reconciling action of God entering into our dialogue with one another and creation, replacing our hearts of stone with hearts of flesh like His. This encounter is conceived in the cave of the heart from which the birth of new life in Christ is born and raises us from the dead even while we are living. Glory to God in the highest place, who visits us in the lowest!

Evlogeson!
Fr Dn Stephen

> + Pray for me the sinner for daring to speak of what
> the Holy Spirit alone can teach through repentance and

---

296 Psalm 63:3.

love in stillness and silence. May God help us to keep
vigil and refuse all suitors but Him until we taste the joy
that does not fade.+

Chapter 7

THE HEART OF PRAYER:
PATRISTIC AND CONTEMPORARY
NEPTIC WITNESSES

N O WORDS ARE QUITE SO HELPFUL in the spiritual search as those born from the wisdom of experience which fly to our hearts on the wings of grace. We all need companions and guides on the Emmaus Way of prayer and the discovery of Christ in our midst. No one should proceed alone, but always be ready to receive and benefit from the cloud of witnesses who have travelled farther than we have, and can be of help in providing direction and confirmation along the Way, the Truth and the Life that is Christ.

Therefore read the words of these witnesses not as one who merely gathers more information, but with focused yearning, as "the hart pants for flowing streams."[297] Prayer that grows by streams of grace from the rich humus of humility cultivated by ascetical struggle, life-long repentance and obedience, yields its noetic savor and fragrance to those hearts which have begun to "taste and see that the Lord is good"[298] and yearn for more. Travel among this field of rare flowers slowly and breathe in deeply the fragrance they yield to all who thirst for the same nectar of divine grace that is our Treasure in earthen vessels.

❧ ❧ ❧

Elder Nikodim of Karoulia

> We pray with the heart. We're aware through the heart.
> But with the mind we only know that we're praying.

---

297 Psalm 42:1.
298 Psalm 34:8.

If I'm praying, I realize—I sense—that I'm praying. I
bring myself to an awareness. Then the feelings become
manifest. And when the feelings appear, then tears flow.
Without consciousness, without feeling, not one little
tear will roll out. If you only know that you're praying to
the Lord, that's one thing. But when it's with the heart,
then you sense that it's the Lord Himself Whom you're
addressing.

*If during prayer a man forgets he's addressing the Lord,
does that mean he's no longer praying with the heart?*

When he addresses Him with his heart, he's praying and has prayer of the heart. But if he doesn't have
the awareness that he's addressing the Lord, then he's
only praying with his head. He knows that there's a
God, and remembers that he's addressing God, but he's
not aware of it. But awareness leads a man to feeling.
And when feeling comes, then he begins to weep. True
repentance is then revealed. He becomes aware of his
sins and begins to repent sincerely. He cries out directly
to the Lord, "Forgive me, forgive me, have mercy on me!"
Everything concludes in the heart. That's how the Lord
created us: He gave us a heart—"our life."[299]

❧❧❧

St. John of Kronstadt

Do you not notice that our heart acts first in our life
and in nearly all our knowledge? The heart sees certain truths (ideas) before the mind knows them. When
knowledge is acquired, it happens thus: the heart sees
at once, indivisibly, instantaneously; afterwards this

299 "Interview with Elder Nikodim of Karoulia" "A Conversation with Elder
Nikodim," *The Orthodox Word.* (Platina, California: St. Herman of Alaska Brotherhood, No 278, 2011) p. 140.

single action of the sight of the heart is transmitted to the intellect and subdivided in the intellect into parts or sections, preceding and subsequent; the sight of the heart is analyzed in the intellect. The idea belongs to the heart and not the intellect; that is to the inner man, and not the outer one. Therefore, to have the eyes of their understanding enlightened (Ephesians 1:18) is a very important matter in acquiring all knowledge, but especially in that of the truths of faith and the laws of morality."[300]

ʚʚʚ

St. Macarius of Egypt

The heart directs all the organs of the body, and when grace gains possession of the heart, it rules over all the members [of the body] and the thoughts. For there, in the heart, the mind abides as well as all the thoughts of the soul and all its hopes. This is how grace penetrates throughout all parts of the body.[301]

For the Greek Fathers, "drawing the mind into the heart" has nothing to do with a surrender to sentimentality. It requires rigorous watchfulness over one's thoughts and feelings rejecting any that are alien to divine grace. However, it is also not simply a process of mental self-correction. There is a real physical connection to be made, one that is only possible because we are *both* physical beings *and* spiritual beings, and

---

300   Saint John of Kronstadt. *My Life In Christ,* Extracts From the Diary of *St. John of Kronstadt* (Archpriest John Iliytch Sergieff) Translated by E. E. Goulaeff, 1984. pp. 47–48.

301   St. Macarius, (trans. George Maloney) *Pseudo-Macarius: The Fifty Spiritual Homilies and the Great Letter* (New York: Paulist Press, (trans. George Maloney) 1992, p. 167.

our spirituality is incomplete if it does not permeate our physical being. This means that the mind and the heart must come to act as one, each in its own proper way responding to divine grace. Then, in the words of St. Macarius, grace will issue from the heart and "penetrate throughout all parts of the body."[302]

ﻉﻉﻉ

St. Gregory Palamas

Our heart is the place of the rational faculty, the first rational organ of the body. Consequently, when we seek to keep watch over and correct our reason by a rigorous sobriety, with what are we to keep watch, if we do not gather together our mind, which has been dissipated abroad by the senses, and lead it back again into the interior, to the selfsame heart which is the seat of the thoughts?

Can you not see, then, how essential it is that those who have determined to pay attention to themselves in inner quiet should gather together the mind and enclose it in the body, and especially in that "body" most interior to the body, which we call the heart?

Has it not occurred to them that the mind is like the eye, which sees other visible objects but cannot see itself? The mind operates in part according to its function of external observation: This is what the great Denys calls the movement of the mind "along a straight line"; and on the other hand, it returns upon itself, when it beholds itself; this movement the same Father

302 Bradshaw, D. "On Drawing the Mind into the Heart: Psychic Wholeness in the Greek Patristic Tradition." Presented at the Sino-American Symposium on Philosophy & Religious Studies, Peking University, July 2006. P10. http://www.uky.edu/~dbradsh/.

calls "circular." This last is the most excellent and most appropriate activity of the mind, by which it comes to transcend itself and be united to God. "For the mind," says St. Basil, "which is not dispersed abroad" (notice how he says "dispersed"? What is dispersed, then, needs to be recollected), "returns to itself, and through itself mounts towards God" as by an infallible road. Denys, that unerring contemplator of intelligible things, says also that this movement of the mind cannot succumb to any error.[303]

❧ ❧ ❧

St. Isaac the Syrian

Purity of mind is one thing, and purity of heart is another, just as a limb differs from the whole body. Now the mind is one of the senses of the soul, but the heart is what contains and holds the inner senses: it is the sense of senses, that is, their root; but if the root is holy, the branches are holy. It is evident, therefore, that if the heart is purified, all the senses are made pure. Now if the mind, on the one hand, is a little diligent in reading the divine Scriptures and toils a little in fasting, vigil, and stillness, it will forget its former activity and will become pure, as long as it abstains from alien concerns. Even so its purity will not be permanent, for just as it is quickly cleansed so too it is quickly soiled.

But the heart, on the other hand, is only made pure by many afflictions, deprivations, separation from all fellowship with the world, and deadness to all things. Once it is purified, however, its purity is not soiled by

303   St. Gregory Palamas. *The Triads On Behalf of the Holy Hesychasts* (Ed. John Meyendorf) (trans. Nicholas Gendle) Mahwah, NJ: Paulist Press, 1983. "The Hesychast method of prayer, and the transformation of the body" Book I, ii, C. p. 38.

little things, nor is it dismayed by great and open conflicts (I mean dreadful ones), inasmuch as it has acquired, as it were, a strong stomach capable of quickly digesting all the food that is indigestible to those who are weak.[304]

᷄᷄᷄

St. Paisios of Mt. Athos

Prayer which is not from the heart, but is made only by the mind, doesn't go any further. To pray with the heart, we must hurt. Just as when we hit our hand or some other part of our body our nous is gathered to the point where we are hurting, so also for the nous to gather in the heart, the heart must hurt. We should make the other's pain our own. We must love the other, must hurt for him, so that we can pray for him. We must come out, little by little, from our own self and begin to love, to hurt for other people.[305]

᷄᷄᷄

Anonymous and hopeless Hagiorite

Inasmuch as a person's heart is not made contrite by prayer, the more he justifies himself and believes himself to be righteous and holy, just as the Pharisee thought himself to be. But when his heart is crushed by the sighs produced by the prayer, his heart is humbled and he sees himself as the Publican.

---

304 *The Ascetical Homilies*, p. 133.
305 Athanasios Rakovalis, *Talks with Father Paisios* (Thessalonica, Greece: Orthodox Kypseli, 2000), pp. 123–24.

Furthermore, a person who has an uncircumcised and self-justified heart does not feel any compunction or genuine reverence for God and divine things upon entering a church, and no heavenly eros comes to him. He stands there in body alone, like a fruitless branch that should be cut off and thrown into the fire, as it is said, "Even now the axe is laid to the root of the trees; every tree therefore that does not bear good fruit is cut down and thrown into the fire." (Lk 3:9) The prayer of such a person arises from a heart completely bereft of warmth and it is spoken in word alone and with a cold intellect. For this reason, such a prayer becomes his condemnation, as it happened with the Pharisee.

The person, however, who has a crushed and humbled heart on account of the force of the prayer, as soon as he enters a church he is immediately arrested and surrounded by a true and vibrant reverence for God and divine things. The divine reverence envelopes him so much that he himself recognizes the energy."[306]

ᏸᏸᏸ

St. Irenaeus of Lyons

Spirits without bodies will never be spiritual men and women. It is our entire being, that is to say, the soul and flesh combined, which by receiving the Spirit of God constitutes the spiritual man.[307]

---

306   A Monk of Mount Athos. *The Watchful Mind: Teachings on the Prayer of the Heart.* Yonkers, NY: St. Vladimir's Seminary Press, 2014, p. 39.

307   Against Heresies. V,8,2 (SC 153 p. 96).

❧❧❧❧

St. Diadochus of Photike

In Hebrew there is no word for the body. The human being is both "animated flesh" and "living soul." (Nobody *has* a soul or *has* flesh.) The flesh denotes the entire human being, but within the limits of creation... The human spirit is not "something," it is this profound "heart," the innermost center where the person gathers and opens the created "flesh" to be vivified by the breath of God. Thus the flesh becomes "spiritual." The heart represents (and partly constitutes) for the Bible and for the ascetics of the Christian East, the innermost center of the individual, the uniquely personal depth called to integrate all of the human faculties in the "sense" of the "sensation of the heart" ... When the "sense of the heart" is reunited through the Spirit, it communicates its joy "to the body itself: in it says the Psalmist, my body has flowered again." So that the man senses God "through the sensation even of his bones."[308]

❧❧❧❧

St. Gregory Palamas

My brother, do you not hear the words of the Apostle, "Our bodies are the temple of the Holy Spirit which is in us," and again, "We are the house of God"? For God Himself says, "I will dwell in them and will walk in them and I shall be their God." So why should anyone who possesses mind grow indignant at the thought that

---

308   As cited by Clement, Olivier, "Life in the Body" *The Ecumenical Review.* World Council of Churches. pp. 128–146.

our mind dwells in that whose nature it is to become
the dwelling place of God? How can it be that God
at the beginning caused the mind to inhabit the body?
Did even He do ill? Rather, brother, such views befit
the heretics, who claim that the body is an evil thing, a
fabrication of the Wicked One.[309]

ৡ৶ ৡ৶ ৡ৶

St. Maximus the Confessor

The whole soul permeates the whole body and gives
it life and motion. At the same time the soul is not
divided or enclosed in it, since the soul is simple and
incorporeal by nature. It is wholly present to the entire
body and to each of its members. The body is of such a
nature that it can make place for the soul by an inherent
power that is receptive to the soul's activity.[310]

ৡ৶ ৡ৶ ৡ৶

Fr. Dumitru Staniloae

This direct knowledge of God seems not to have been
understood in the East as a knowledge belonging to
a mind that is separated from the body and from the
world, but as that of a mind sensitive to the fact of life
in the body and sensitive to the entirety of experience
in the world. This is the direct knowledge proper to the

---

309   St. Gregory Palamas. *The Triads On Behalf of the Holy Hesychasts* (Ed. John
Meyendorf) (trans. Nicholas Gendle) Mahwah, NJ: Paulist Press, 1983. "The Hesychast method of prayer, and the transformation of the body" Book I, ii, C. p. 40.
310   *Ambigua*, 7, PG 91 1100AB cited by Larchet, Jean-Claude, *Mental Disorders and Spiritual Healing*, New York: Sophia Perennis, p. 25.

mind of a purified body, a mind that feels the effect of purification in its relation to the world. It is a direct knowledge that arises through the medium of a world that has become transparent.[311]

The intimate insertion of the soul into body and its characterization as incarnate spirit or soul from the first moment of its existence does not mean that the soul cannot exist after death and before the resurrection of the body in virtue of the fact that it is no longer in the body. The soul carries with it its characterization as soul of the body and has the roots of the body deepened within itself during the course of life on earth. This, too, shows that the soul is a factor distinct from the body, yet without it ever being pure spirit only and hence receiving no qualities via the body with which it lived in a certain time and space.[312]

❧❧❧

Panayiotis Nellas

The directions from the Lenten Triodion on how the *Great Canon of St. Andrew of Crete* is to be sung describe not merely the ritual but also the general anthropological and cosmological context in which the service is celebrated. The rubrics define the conditions under which prayer can be real, effective and fruitful, that is, the setting within which a person can concentrate all the aspects of his existence—intellect, will, conscience, emotions, senses, body—on God and, by adhering to

---

311 Staniloae, D. *The Experience of God: Orthodox Dogmatic Theology, Vol. II. The World: Creation and Deification*, Brookline, MA: Holy Cross Orthodox Press, pp. 77–78.

312 Ibid., pp. 80–81.

Him constantly and laboriously, can purify them, integrate and illuminate them, and so offer them to God and unite them with Him.[313]

ᔒᔒᔒ

St. Isaac the Syrian

Whenever you find it delightful to kneel [in prayer], do not be carried off [by the thought] to put an end to it. Whenever your mind is concentrated do not cut off your prayer.

Do not count as idleness the protraction of wandering concentrated prayer because you abandon the psalms [*for the sake of it*]. More than the practice of psalmody, love prostrations during prayer. When prayer gives you her hand she will take the place of your office. And when the very time of your office you are granted the gift of tears, do not count the delight, which you find in them as an interruption of your liturgy. For the fullness of prayer is the gift of tears.[314]

After a time, a certain sweetness is born in the heart from the practice of this labor [of remaining silent], and it leads the body by force to persevere in stillness. A multitude of tears is born to us in this discipline through a wonderful divine vision of something that the heart distinctly perceives, sometimes with pain, sometimes with amazement. For the heart humbles herself and becomes

---

313 Panayiotis Nellas (1987) *Deification in Christ: Orthodox Perspectives on the Nature of the Human Person*. St. Vladimir's Press: New York. Pp 163–164.

314 *The Ascetical Homilies of St. Isaac the Syrian*, Revised second edition. Trans. From the Greek and Syriac, Holy Transfiguration Monastery, Boston, MA, 2011, Homily 64, p. 449.

like a tiny babe, and as soon as she begins to pray, tears flow forth in advance of her prayer.[315]

❧ ❧ ❧

St. Symeon the New Theologian

He who does not have attention in himself and does not guard his mind, cannot become pure in heart and so cannot see God. He who does not have attention in himself cannot be poor in spirit, cannot weep and be contrite, nor be gentle and meek, nor hunger and thirst after righteousness, nor be merciful, nor a peacemaker, nor suffer persecution for righteousness sake.[316]

❧ ❧ ❧

Elder Sophrony of Essex

Each and every kind of mental activity presents less of a strain than prayer. We may be capable of working for ten or twelve hours on end but a few moments of prayer and we are exhausted.[317]

The practice of mental prayer may for a while be associated with the hesychastic method—in other words, it may take the form of rhythmic or a-rhythmic articulation of the prayer as described, by breathing in during the first half and breathing out during the second part. This can be genuinely helpful if one does not lose sight of the fact that every invocation of the Name of Christ must be inseparably coupled with a consciousness of

315   Ibid., p. 453.
316   E. Kadloubovsky and G.E.H. Palmer, trans. *Writings from the Philokalia on Prayer of the Heart* (London: Faber and Faber, 1951), p. 158.
317   Archimandrite Sophrony, *His Life Is Mine*, St. Vladimir's Seminary press, Crestwood NY 1977. pp. 55–56.

Christ Himself. The Name must not be detached from the Person of God, lest prayer be reduced to a technical exercise and so contravene the commandment, "Thou shalt not take the name of the Lord thy God in vain" (Exod. 20:7; Deut. 5:11).[318]

True prayer comes exclusively through faith and repentance accepted as the only foundation. The danger of psychotechnics is that not a few of us attribute too great significance to method *qua* method. In order to avoid such deformation the beginner should follow another practice, which, though considerably slower is incomparably better and more wholesome—to fix attention on the Name of Jesus Christ and on the words of the prayer. When contrition for sin reaches a certain level, the mind naturally heeds the heart.[319]

ع ع ع

St. Gregory Palamas

When someone is striving to concentrate his intellect in himself so that it functions, not according to the direct form of movement but according to the circular, delusion-free form, how could he not gain immensely if instead of letting his gaze flit hither and thither, he fixes it upon his chest or his navel as upon a point of support? ... 'Be attentive to yourself,' says Moses (Deut. 15:9. LXX) - that is, *to the whole of yourself,* [emphasis added] not to a few things that pertain to you, neglecting the rest. By what means? With the intellect (*nous*) assuredly, for nothing else can pay attention to the whole of yourself. Set this guard, therefore, over your

---

318 Sophrony, A. *On Prayer*, p. 143.
319 Ibid., p. 142.

soul and body, for thereby you will readily free yourself
from the evil passions of body and soul. Take yourself in
hand, then, be attentive to yourself, scrutinize yourself;
or, rather, guard, watch over and test yourself, for in this
manner you will subdue your rebellious unregenerate
self to the Spirit and there will never again be "some
secret iniquity in your heart" (Deut. 15:9). If, says, the
Preacher, the spirit that rules over the evil demons and
passions rises up against you, do not desert your place
(cf., Eccles. 10:4)—that is to say, *do not leave any part
of your soul or body unwatched* [emphasis added]. In this
way you will master the evil spirits that assail you and
you will boldly present yourself to Him who examines
hearts and minds (cf. Ps. 7:9); and He will not scrutinize you, for you will have already scrutinized yourself.
As St. Paul says, "If we judged ourselves we would not
be judged" (1 Cor. 11:31).[320]

᳘᳘᳘

St. Hesychius the Priest

An intellect that does not neglect its inner struggle will
find that ... the five bodily senses, too, are freed from
all external evil influences... It withdraws the senses
almost completely into itself.[321]

---

320 *The Philokalia, Volume Four,* Faber and Faber, 1995, pp. 338–339.
321   St. Hesychius the priest, *Philokalia, Vol 1,* .53 On Watchfulness and Holiness, pp.171–172.

ᕤᕤᕤᕤ

St. Maximos the Confessor

Sense perception allied with the activity of the intellect produces virtue with spiritual knowledge ... (but) when the senses have the intellect in their clutches, they propagate polytheism through each individual sense organ; because in their slavery to the passions they pay divine honors to the sensible objects corresponding to each organ.[322]

ᕤᕤᕤᕤ

St. Porphyrios

In our prayer we should ask only for the salvation of our soul. Didn't the Lord say, *Seek first the Kingdom of God, and all these things will be added to you?* Easily, without the slightest difficulty, Christ can give us what we want. And remember the secret. The secret is not to think about asking for the specific thing at all. The secret is to ask for your union with Christ with utter selflessness, without saying, "give me this," or "give me that." It suffices to say, *"Lord Jesus Christ, have mercy on me."* God has no need to be informed by us about our various needs. He knows them all incomparably better than we do and He gives us His love. What is important is for us to respond to this love with prayer and with the keeping of His commandments. We should ask for the will of God to be done. That is what is in our best interest and the safest thing for us and for those for whom we pray.

---

322 *The Philokalia, Vol. I*, pp. 251, 254.

Christ will give us everything abundantly. When there is even a trace of egotism, nothing happens.[323]

❧ ❧ ❧

Elder Ephraim of Kotounakia

How should we say the Jesus prayer, Elder? Should we say the entire phrase, "Lord Jesus Christ, Son of God, have mercy on me?"

No, no, this is tiring. It suffices to just say the words, "Lord Jesus Christ, have mercy upon me." If you progress in prayer, you will omit other words, too, because of the desire in your soul. You will probably end up saying just "Jesus, have mercy upon me" or "Sweetest Jesus, have mercy upon me." You will be crying out full of yearning, only the name "Jesus, Jesus…" If you are blessed to still progress, then you will find yourself absolutely speechless, as if in rapture, feeling the fervor of divine grace.

We start the Jesus prayer in a whisper or loudly until our mind is collected and starts paying attention to the prayer. Then we pray inwardly, without whispering. Everyone learns this by experience. As for the mood, if we do not have it, then we create it. We bring to mind some spiritual images that may touch the soul; for example the Crucifixion of the Lord…or the Second Coming.

So Elder, should we have such images in mind while repeating the prayer?

No, no. We use thought [images] only in the beginning just to warm up the soul. When we say the Jesus

---

323 St. Porphyrios, *Wounded by Love, the Life and the Wisdom of Elder Porphyrios*, Greece: Denise Harvey, p. 116.

prayer we say it slowly and consciously. We have nothing on our mind, neither words, nor faces, or even images.

Should we pray with improvised words, Elder?

I do it quite often. The improvised prayer, as well as the spiritual images and visions we mentioned previously help the soul reach a state of grace; even the quietest chant, hymn, or spontaneous words, may help the soul reach high spiritual states. In that case, we do not need all these things; we put them aside and pray just by saying the Jesus prayer with ardor, "Lord Jesus Christ, have mercy upon me." Other times, when we are in a good spiritual state, we yearn to chant from the bottom of our heart; or when our soul is suddenly filled with spiritual thoughts, we wish to improvise our prayer. Then, we should let our soul quench its thirst.

So is this mental prayer Elder? Should we control our breathing when we practice it?

No, this is the beginning of mental [noetic] prayer. Mental prayer itself is an act of the holy grace. When the soul is ready, then God promotes it to the perfection of mental prayer. Until then, we ought to pray by repeating the Jesus prayer, always having obedience as our firm foundation. One's breathing does not necessarily have to be connected to prayer. This is a secondary element. More importantly, prayer should not be related to the heartbeat, but rather with the place of the heart; not with the heartbeat, no.[324]

---

324 *Elder Ephraim of Katounakia,* Mount Athos, Greece: H. Hesychasterion of St. Ephraim, 2003 pp.121–124.

ð❧ ð❧ ð❧

Abbot Haralambos Dionysiatis

You ask why I suggest you say the prayer standing, although it says in patristic books that it's better to concentrate when sitting on a small stool. The stool is good. However, it's not for you. Not even for me, who is getting close to old age. I notice that when I say the prayer standing, the prayer flows quickly and purely. It brings compunction, tears, contemplation, and other things, which you can't understand now. Many times, so much fragrance comes from the chest that even the cell smells fragrant.[325] The same thing happens with Elder Arsenios. Did you see that old Elder? If only you knew what grace he has! At such an age and yet, many times, he feels such a sweetness when he prays and such fragrance that he forgets himself and remains standing for hours on end. The opposite happens with Father Prodromos. Even though he is young, when he gets tired standing up, his mind becomes muddled. However, sitting on a stool, he is able to concentrate so much on the prayer that he has even happened to reach the state of ecstasy.

That's why I emphasize to you again the it's imperative you have a suitable guide. For the young, particularly, to be able to concentrate it is imperative that they first subdue the body with toils, prostrations, fasting according to one's strength, and by standing, as much

---

325 Witnesses have repeatedly noticed strong fragrance accompanying the holy prayers of the elder and others like him. Evagrius the Solitary (in *The Philokalia*, Vol. I. p. 70.) writes, "So long as you have not renounced the passions, and your intellect is still opposed to holiness and truth, you will not find the fragrance of incense in your breast." St. Niketas Stethatos writes, "When you come to participate in the Holy Spirit and recognize His presence through a certain ineffable energy and fragrance within yourself—this fragrance even spreading over the surface of your body—you can no longer be content to remain within the bounds of the created world." (From *The Philokalia*, Vol. 4. p.149.)

as possible. Try on your own, if you want to see the difference. As for kneeling, this happens sometimes from much contrition. As the struggler sees Christ, with the eyes of his heart, he feels the need to fall down. His knees give way; he can't cope. He falls at the Lord' feet. However, be careful, many times the devil makes the knees bend in order to bring negligence and sleep.

However, when you get tired standing, it is good that, instead of sitting down comfortably, you alternate the prayer so that it is sometimes said standing, sometimes kneeling and sometimes even sitting. When we don't have the strength, God provides for us whether we stand, or kneel, or sit; even when we lie in bed we can pray. However, if you have the physical ability, the devil doesn't joke around, he immediately brings on negligence, muddling of the mind, and sleep. Many strugglers even get used to saying the prayer while walking in order to fight off negligence and sleep.[326]

ﺒﻳ ﺒﻳ ﺒﻳ

St. Dorotheos of Gaza

If a man really sets his heart upon the will of God, God will enlighten a little child to tell that man what is His will. But if a man does not truly desire the will of God, even if he goes in search of a prophet, God will put into the heart of the prophet a reply like the deception in his own heart.[327]

---

326 Monk Joseph. *Abbot Haralambos Dionysiatis, The Teacher of Noetic Prayer,* Athens, Greece: H. Monastery Dionysiou, pp. 218–219.

327 St. *Dorotheos of Gaza, Discourses and Sayings,* Kalamazoo, MI: Cistercian Publications, 1977, p. 129.

ৰ৶ ৰ৶ ৰ৶

St. Isaac the Syrian

A man who sits in stillness and receives experience of
God's kindness has little need of persuasive argument,
and his soul is not sick with the disease of unbelief,
like those who are doubtful of the truth. For the testimony of his own understanding is sufficient to persuade
him above endless words having no experience behind
them.[328]

ৰ৶ ৰ৶ ৰ৶

Met. Anthony Bloom

God meets a human being at the level of his soul, that
is, ultimately at the level of silence and of those things
which are beyond words, at the level of mystery, of those
things which can be known within silence but which
cannot be expressed by words otherwise than symboli-
cally, which can only be hinted at… Ultimately, a meeting between a soul and God takes place at the heart
of silence. Any meeting between two persons takes
place beyond words. *It takes place where God is* [empha-
sis added]. When the time comes when all things are
fulfilled, we will not meet on the level of our psychological richness or poverty, we will meet spirit to spirit
and soul to soul. And on this earth we need to be aware
of it… In a way, real communication begins where the

328 Homily 68, *The Ascetical Homilies of St. Isaac the Syrian,* Revised second
edition. Trans. From the Greek and Syriac, Holy Transfiguration Monastery, Boston,
MA, 2011, p. 480.

ordinary means of communication have been left aside. Real understanding is beyond words.[329]

ə♪ ə♪ ə♪

St. Makarios of Egypt

Some repose in God's grace only for as long as they can keep a hold over themselves and can avoid being vanquished by the sinfulness dwelling within them: for a time, they can pray diligently and are at rest, but then unclean thoughts become active within them and they are taken captive by sin, which in their case clearly coexists with grace. Those who are superficial, and who have not yet grasped the precise degree to which divine energy is active in them, think they have been delivered once and for all from sin; but those who are intelligent and possess discrimination would not deny that, though God's grace dwells within them, they may also be harassed by shameful and unnatural thoughts.

We have often known brethren who have enjoyed such richness of grace that all sinful desire has completely dried up and been extinguished in them for five or six years. Then, just when they thought they had reached a haven and found peace, evil has leapt upon them as though from an ambush so savagely and such hostility that they have been thrown into confusion and doubt. No one, therefore, who possesses understanding would dare to say that once grace dwells in him he is thereafter free from sin. As we said, both grace and sin may be active in the same intellect, even if the gullible and ignorant, after having had some slight

---

329 Anthony Bloom, "The Suffering and Death of Children" *Sourozh*, No. 9, 1984.

spiritual experience, claim that they have already won the battle.[330]

❧❧❧

St. Symeon the New Theologian

On one occasion when [St Symeon the New Theologian] was standing in pure prayer and conversing with God, he saw with his intellect the air start to shimmer and although he was inside his cell, he seemed to be outside, in the open air. It was nighttime about the first watch. As it began to get light overhead like the glimmer of daybreak…the building and everything else disappeared and he seemed no longer to be inside. While he was in this state of complete ecstasy and was contemplating with his whole intellect the light that was appearing, it gradually increased. It made the air seem brighter, and he felt himself and his whole body transcending this earthly existence. The light continued to get brighter and brighter and seemed to be shining down on him from above like the sun at midday. As it did so he felt himself standing in the midst of this manifestation and his whole body was completely filled with joy and tears from the sweetness that emanated from it.

Then he saw the light *taking hold of his flesh in a strange way and gradually merging into his limbs* [emphasis added]. The strangeness of this sight distracted him from his earlier vision and caused him to contemplate only what was happening within him in this completely extraordinary way. Thus he watched until little by little, the light was imparted to his whole body, to his heart, and his internal organs, and rendered him wholly fire

---

330   *The Philokalia*, Vol III, 75.76. 1984. p. 318.

and light. And just as had happened before with the building, so now it caused him to lose awareness of the form, the structure, the mass, and the shape of his body, and he stopped weeping. Then a voice came to him from out of the light saying, "This is how it has been determined that the holy ones *who are alive* and *who remain* are to be transformed *at* the last *trumpet*, and in this state *caught up* as St. Paul says.[331]

After many hours standing in this fashion…he began to think and say to himself, "Will I revert to my previous bodily form or am I going to stay like this?" As he was wondering about this, all of a sudden he realized that he was still carrying his bodily form around with him like a shadow or some immaterial substance. For when, as I have said, he felt himself, along with his body, becoming wholly light that was immaterial and without shape or form, he knew that his body was still joined to him, although it was somehow incorporeal and spiritual in some way. For he had the sense that it now had no weight or solidity, and he was amazed to see himself as though he were incorporeal when he still had his body. But then again the light, with the same voice as before, spoke within him and said, "After the resurrection in the age to come, this is how all the saints will be incorporeally clothed with spiritual bodies. These will either be lighter, subtler, and floating higher in the air, or more solid, heavier, and sinking down toward the ground, and by this means each will have their station, rank, and intimacy with God established at that time.[332]

---

331 St. Niketas Stethatos, *The Life of Saint Symeon the New Theologian*, (Richard Greenfield, trans.) Dumbarton Oaks Medieval Library, Cambridge, Mass: Harvard University Press, 2013, pp 155, 157.

332 Ibid, p. 159.

ઝ૭ ઝ૭ ઝ૭

St. Niphon, Bishop of Constantia

Then there came a profound silence. The eyes of St.
Niphon received a pure, unmixed light so he could see.
The first angelic host, which surrounded the banquet,
was assigned to perform an uninterrupted and unending
song. It was overcome with an unspeakable and unspoken joy. Immediately the divine and awesome angelic
choir began an unspeakable doxology. The hearts of the
saints leaped with joy and delight. From the first angelic
choir the magnificent song of doxology went on to the
second host, the seraphim. It then began to sing a mys-
tical song with great artistry. The doxology resounded
like a sevenfold sweetness in the ears of the saints, who
rejoiced unspeakably with all their senses. Their *eyes saw*
the unapproachable light, *they smelled the scent* of the
fragrance of Divinity, *their ears heard* the divine song
of the all-holy Powers, *their mouth tasted the Body and
Blood of the Lord Jesus Christ* anew in the Kingdom of
Heaven, *their hands felt eternal good things* and *their feet
danced* to the sound of the feast. Thus *all their senses were
filled with unspeakable joy.* [emphasis added] After a little while the second angelic host passed the divine song
on to the third, the fourth, and on to the last angelic
choir, creating pleasure and joy in the hearts of the saints
with the sweetness of the song. And it was amazing that
the angelic hosts did not continuously sing the same
song, but there was an unbounded variety of songs and
newness in the songs they sang. When the seven circles
of angelic hosts had completed their all-holy doxology,
the choir of the Archangels began to sing the Trisagion:
Michael sang and Gabriel responded; then Raphael
sang and Uriel responded. An extraordinary harmony

was heard. The four pillars of fire, the Archangels, were elevated above all; their song was flaming and piercing.

Moved by the unspeakable sweetness, all the saints at the heavenly banquet then began to sing the greatness of God. Thus the angelic song resounded everywhere, within and without – the all-holy song which enflamed the holy hearts with a joyful pleasure unto endless ages. After he had seen all this three times, Blessed Niphon, being in a great ecstasy of vision, heard the voice of God telling him, "Niphon, Niphon, your prophetic vision was beautiful. Write down in detail all that you have seen and heard, for this is what will come to pass. And I have showed these things to you because you are My faithful friend, My beloved son and heir of My kingdom. So rest assured, now that I have vouchsafed you to see these awesome mysteries, of My great love for those who humbly worship My Kingdom and Dominion. For I rejoice to look upon the meek and humble one who trembles at My words."

After He had said these things, the Lord delivered him from that awesome and most wondrous vision, which had held him in its grip for two weeks. When he came to himself he was filled with dread and sighed with sorrow. His tears flowed in torrents...[333]

---

333 Arhim. Petroniu Tănase, *Viaţa şi învăţăturile Sfântului Ierarh Nifon*, Editura Episcopiei Romanului şi Huşilor, ("The Vision of the Awesome Judgment" from the hagiography of St. Niphon, Bishop of Constantia, trans. Fr. David Hudson), 1993, reeditat 2001, p. 109.

One should remember God more often than one breathes[334]

---

334 Evagrius, Kadloubovsky, E. and Palmer, G.E.H. (eds.) *Early Fathers from the Philokalia.* Faber and Faber Limited: London, 1976. p. 113.

ABOUT THE AUTHOR

Fr. Dn. Stephen Muse, Ph.D, LMFT, LPC is Director of Education and Counselor Training and the Clergy-in-Kairos week-long intensive stress and wellness program for clergy (and their spouses) at the Pastoral Institute in Columbus, Georgia. He taught and supervised U.S. Army and Air Force Family Life Chaplains for 21 years and has worked extensively with combat veterans and their families after deployment and persons healing from trauma, grief and spiritual pain.

He is a past president of the Orthodox Christian Association of Medicine, Psychology and Religion; serves on the Pastoral Praxis Committee of the Assembly of Canonical Orthodox Bishops and as an advisor to the Orthodox Church of America's task force on spiritual abuse. He is founder of the Holy Transfiguration Greek Orthodox Church Mission in Columbus, GA where he served as the first Parish Council President and now as a deacon. He and his wife Claudia have been married for 35 years and have four children and four grandchildren.

Fr. Dn. Stephen holds Diplomate certification in the American Association of Pastoral Counselors, in Professional Psychotherapy with the International Academy of Behavioral Medicine, Counseling and Psychotherapy and with the American Academy of Experts in Traumatic Stress. He is an AAMFT Approved supervisor, Certified Professional Counseling Supervisor, EAGALA certified in Equine Assisted Therapy, National Board Certified in clinical hypnotherapy, EMDR II qualified, a Certified Clinical Mental Health Counselor and State licensed in Georgia as a Professional Counselor and Marriage and Family Therapist.

Books by the author
- ***Beside Still Waters: Restoring the Souls of Shepherds in the Market Place*** (Smyth & Helwys, Georgia, 2000)

- *Raising Lazarus: Integral Healing in Orthodox Christianity*, (Holy Cross, Brookline, MA, 2004)
- *When Hearts Become Flame: An Eastern Orthodox Approach to the διά-Λογος of Pastoral Counseling.* New Hampshire: ORI, 2011 (Greek Edition 2014, Athens, Greece: Editions Gregory, 2015; 2nd edition, Revised, Waymart, PA: St. Tikhon's Monastery Press, 2016)
- **Being Bread**, (New Hampshire, ORI, 2013; Waymart, PA: St. Tikhon's Monastery Press, 2016)
- *The Peddler and the Disenchanted Mirror* (Parrisia Editions, Greece, 2016; American and Kindle editions, 2016)
- ΝΑ ΕΙΣΑΙ Ο ΕΑΥΤΟΣ ΣΟΥ Ὅπως ἔκανε ο Αμίμ *[BECOME YOURSELF like Amim did], EnPloEditions, Greece, 2016)*
- *Caregivers as Confessors & Healers,* (Stephen Muse, PhD, James Burg, PhD, Helena Woroncow, MD, eds.) Wichita, Kansas: Eighth Day Institute. 2016.
- *Become Yourself (Amim's Great Discovery!)* Waymart, PA: St. Tikhon's Monastery Press, 2017.

BIBLIOGRAPHY

Aimilianos, A. *The Way of the Spirit: Reflections on Life in God*. Greece: Indiktos, 2009.

Balan, I. *Elder Cleopa of Sihastria*, Lake George, CO: New Varatec Publishing, 2001.

Bloom, A. *Beginning to Pray*. New York: Paulist Press, 1970.

Bloom, A. "The Suffering and Death of Children" *Sourozh*, No. 9, 1984.

Bradshaw, D. "On Drawing the Mind into the Heart: Psychic Wholeness in the Greek Patristic Tradition." Presented at the Sino-American Symposium on Philosophy & Religious Studies, Peking University, July 2006.

Bunge, G. *Dragon's Wine and Angel's Bread: The Teaching of Evagrius Ponticus on Anger and Meekness*. Crestwood, NY: St. Vladimir's Seminary Press, 2009.

Cardenal, E. *Love: A Glimpse of Eternity*, Massachusetts: Paraclete Press, 2006.

Chrysostomos, A. *A Guide to Orthodox Psychotherapy: The Science, Theology and Spiritual Practice Behind It and Its Clinical Application*, University Press of America, 2007.

Clement of Alexandria, *Stromata (Miscellanies)* Early Christian Writings, Orthodox E Books. http://www.earlychristianwritings.com/text/clement-stromata-book1.html.

Clement, Olivier, "Life in the Body" *The Ecumenical Review*. World Council of Churches. 33(2) 1981, pp. 128-146.

Clement, O. *The Roots of Christian Mysticism: Texts From the Patristic Era with Commentary*, New York: New City Press. 1993.

Climacus, St. John *The Ladder of Divine Ascent.* Mahwah, NJ: Paulist Press, 1982.

Deseille, P. *Orthodox Spirituality and the Philokalia.* (A. Gythiel, trans.) Wichita, KA: Eighth Day Press, 2008.

St. Dorotheos of Gaza, Discourses and Sayings, (Wheeler, E, ed.), Kalamazoo, MI: Cistercian Publications, 1977.

Ephraim, A. "The Sinlessness of Our Most Holy Lady," *Analogia*, Athens, Greece: St. Maxim the Greek Institute, No. 1, September, 2016.

Ephraim, Elder, *Counsels From the Holy Mountain*, Florence, AZ: St. Anthony's Monastery, 1999.

Ephraim, E. *Elder Ephraim of Katounakia.* (trans. T. Vassiliadou-Christodoulou), Mt. Athos, Greece: H. Hesychaste-rion "Saint Ephraim," 2003.

Saint-Exupéry, Antoine de, *The Little Prince*, New York: Harcourt Books, 2000.

Felmy, K.C., *Ortodoxe Theologie. Der Gegenwart. Eine Einführung*, εκδ. Wissenschaftliche Buchgesellschaft, Darmstadt, 1990.

Florovsky, G. *Bible, Church, Tradition: An Eastern Orthodox View* (Volume 1 in the *Collected Works of Georges Florovsky*). Belmont, MA: Nordland Publishing, 1987.

St. Irenaeus, *Against the Heresies* in The Ante-Nicene Fathers, (Roberts and Donaldson, trans.) Michigan: Eerdmans Publishing Company, 1950.

St. Isaac the Syrian, *The Ascetical Homilies of St. Isaac the Syrian* revised second edition. Trans. From the Greek and Syriac, Holy Transfiguration Monastery, Boston, MA, 2011.

John, Fr. *Christ Is In Our Midst: Letters from a Russian Monk.* Crestwood, NY: St. Vladimir's Seminary Press, 1980.

Saint John of Kronstadt. *My Life In Christ* Extracts From the Diary of *St. John of Kronstadt* (Archpriest John Iliytch Sergieff) Translated by E. E. Goulaeff, 1984.

Kadloubovsky, E. and Palmer, G.E.H. (eds.) *Writings From the Philokalia on Prayer of the Heart,* London: Faber & Faber, 1975.

Kadloubovsky, E. and Palmer, G.E.H. (eds.) *Early Fathers from the Philokalia.* Faber and Faber Limited: London, 1976.

Karakolis, C. "The Mother of Jesus in the Gospel According to John: A Narrative-Critical and Theological Perspective." *Analogia,* Athens, Greece: St. Maxim the Greek Institute, No. 1, September, 2016, pp. 1–15.

Keselopoulos, A. *Passions and Virtues According to Saint Gregory Palamas.* St. Tikhon's Seminary Press: South Canaan, Pennsylvania, 2004.

Kittel, G. (ed.) *Theological Dictionary of the New Testament. Vol II.* Grand Rapids, Michigan: Wm. B. Eerdmans Publishing Co. 1964.

Laird, Martin. *Into the Silent Land: A Guide to the Christian Practice of Contemplation.* Oxford University Press: England, 2006.

Lampe, G. W. H. *A Patristic Greek Lexicon.* England: Oxford University Press, 1969.

Larchet, Jean-Claude, *Mental Disorders and Spiritual Healing,* New York: Sophia Perennis, 2005

Larchet, Jean-Claude, *Therapy of Spiritual Illnesses: An Introduction to the Ascetic Tradition of the Orthodox Church.* Vols. I-III. (Kilian Sprecher, trans.) Vol. 1, Montreal, Canada: Alexander Press, 2012.

Loudovikos, N, *Hell and Heaven, Nature and Person. Chr. Yannaras, D. Stăniloae and Maximus the Confessor Holiness: The Sacrament of Surprise, International Journal of Orthodox Theology* 5:1 (2014) urn:nbn:de:0276-2014-1027.

St. Macarius, (trans. George Maloney) *Pseudo-Macarius: The Fifty Spiritual Homilies and the Great Letter,* New York: Paulist Press, (trans. George Maloney) 1992.

Maximus the Confessor, *On the Difficulties in the Church Fathers, The Ambigua,* Vol. I. (trans. Nicholas Constas), Cambridge, MA: Harvard University Press, 2014.

Metallinos, G. *The Way: An Introduction to the Christian Faith, http:// www.oodegr.co/english/biblia/Metallinos_The_Way/contents.htm,* created 23/8/2010.

A Monk of Mount Athos, *The Watchful Mind.* Yonkers, NY: St. Vladimir's Seminary Press. 2014.

Monk Joseph. *Abbot Haralambos Dionysiatis, The Teacher of Noetic Prayer,* Athens, Greece: H. Monastery Dionysiou.

Muse, S, "No Dead Man's Prayer," *Touchstone,* Mar/April, 2013.

Muse, S. *When the Heart Becomes Flame: An Eastern Orthodox Approach to the dia-Logos of Pastoral Counseling, 2nd edition,* Waymart, PA: St. Tikhon's Monastery Press, 2015.

Nellas, Panayiotis, *Deification in Christ.* Crestwood, NY: St. Vladimir's Seminary Press, 1987.

Needleman, J. *Lost Christianity.* New York: Doubleday & Company, Inc. 1980.

Nesteruk, A. *Light from the East: Theology, science, and the Eastern Orthodox Tradition.* Minneapolis: Fortress Press, 2003.

Elder Nikodim of Karoulia. "A Conversation with Elder Nikodim," *The Orthodox Word.* (Platina, California: St. Herman of Alaska Brotherhood, No 278, 2011.

St. Gregory Palamas. *The Triads On Behalf of the Holy Hesychasts* (Ed. John Meyendorff) (trans. Nicholas Gendle) Mahwah, NJ: Paulist Press, 1983.

Paisius, St. *Spiritual Struggle.* Souroti, Greece: Holy Monastery of St. John the Theologian, 2010.

Palmer, G.E.H., Sherrard, P., Ware, K. (eds.) *The Philokalia.* Vols. I-IV, 1979–1995.

Papacioc, Archimandrite Arsenie "Eternity Hidden in the Moment" The Orthodox Word. (St. Herman of Alaska: California, 2011) No. 281.

Pert, C. *Molecules of Emotion: The Science Behind Mind-Body Medicine.* Simon & Schuster: New York, 1999.

Roberts, A. and Donaldson, J., eds. Ante-Nicene Fathers: Translations of the Writings of the Fathers Down to A.D. 325., Grand Rapids, Michigan: Eerdmans, Pub. Co., 1956.

St. Porphyrios, *Wounded by Love, the Life and the Wisdom of Elder Porphyrios,* Greece: Denise Harvey, 2005.

St. Porphyrios. *Life and Words* (Greek) Trans. Holy Monastery of Pantokrator, Holy Monastery of Chrisopigi of Chania, 2003.

St. Niketos Stethatos, *The Life of Saint Symeon the New Theologian,* (Richard Greenfield, trans.) Dumbarton Oaks Midieval Library, Cambridge, Mass: Harvard University Press, 2013.

Prayer Book for Orthodox Christians. Holy Transfiguration Monastery: Boston, 2000.

Rakovalis, Athanasios, *Talks with Father Paisios,* Thessaloniki: Greece: Orthodox Kypseli, 2000.

Romanides, Fr. John, *Patristic Theology,* Thessaloniki, Greece: Uncut Mountain Press, 2008.

Rossi, A. *Becoming a Healing Presence,* Chesterton, Indiana: Ancient Faith Publishing, 2014.

Schmemann, A. *The journals of father Alexander Schmemann 1973–1983 (trans.* Juliana Schmemann) St. Vladimir's Seminary Press. Crestwood NY, 2002.

Schmemann, A. *O Death, Where Is Thy Sting?* Crestwood, NY: St. Vladimir's Seminary Press, 2003.

Sophrony. A. St. *Silouan the Athonite.* Essex, England: St. John the Baptist Stavropegic Monastery, 1991.

Sophrony, A. *Words of Life,* Essex: Stavropegic Monastery of St. John the Baptist, 1996.

Sophrony, A. *On Prayer,* Crestwood, NY: St. Vladimir's Seminary Press, 1996

Sophrony, A. *His Life Is Mine,* trans. Rosemary Edmonds, Crestwood, NY: St. Vladimir's, 1997.

Sophrony, A. *We Shall See Him As He Is.* Alaska: St. Herman of Alaska Brotherhood, 2006.

Sophrony. A. *Letters To His Family,* Essex, England: Stavropegic Monastery of St. John the Baptist, 2015.

Sophrony, A. *Striving For The Knowledge of God, Letters to David Balfour,* Essex, England: Stavropegic Monastery of St. John the Baptist, 2016.

Sherrard, P. *The Eclipse of Man and Nature: An Enquiry into the Origins and Consequences of Modern Science.* Vermont: Inner Traditions/Lindisfarne Press, 1987.

Stamoulis, C. Θεοτόκος και ορθόδοξο δόγμα. Σπουδή στη διδασκαλία του αγίου Κυρίλλου Αλεξανδρείας Θεσσαλονίκη, Ελλάδα: εκδ. Το Παλίμψηστον, 2003.

Stamoulis. Έρως και θάνατος. Δοκιμή για έναν πολιτισμό της σάρκωσης, Athens, Greece: Akritas publications, 2009.

Staniloae, D. *The Experience of God: Orthodox Dogmatic Theology, Vol. I. The Experience of God*, Brookline, MA: Holy Cross Orthodox Press, 1998.

Staniloae, D. *The Experience of God: Orthodox Dogmatic Theology, Vol. II. The World: Creation and Deification*, Brookline, MA: Holy Cross Orthodox Press, 2005.

Elder Thaddeus of Vitovnica, *Our Thoughts Determine Our Lives*. St. Herman of Alaska Brotherhood, 2009.

Tikhon, A. *Everyday Saints and Other Stories*, Moscow, Russia: Pokrov Publications, 2012.

Vasiljevic, M. *History, Truth, Holiness: Studies in Theological Ontology and Epistemology*, Alhambra, CA: Sebastian Press, 2011

Vasileios, A. *The Parable of the Prodigal Son*, Quebec, Canada: Alexander Press, 1996.

Veniamin, Christopher (trans.) *Saint Gregory Palamas the Homilies*. Pennsylvania: Mount Thabor Publishing, 2014.

Vlachos, M. "The Annunciation of the Virgin Mary," http://www.orthodoxchristian.info/pages/annunciation.htm

Webber, M. *Bread & Water, Wine & Oil*, Indiana: Conciliar Press, 2007.

Williams, M. *The Velveteen Rabbit*, New York: Doubleday, 1991.

Zacharias, A. *Remember Thy First Love: The Three Stages of the Spiritual Life in the Theology of Elder Sophrony*. Mount Thabor Publishing: Pennsylvania, 2010.

Zacharias, Archimandrite, *Man the Target of God*. Stavropegic Monastery of St. John the Baptist: Essex, 2015.

Zizioulas, J. *Being as Communion: Studies in Personhood and the Church*. New York: St. Vladimir's Seminary Press, 1997.

Zizioulas, J. *Communion and Otherness: Further Studies in Personhood and the Church*, New York: Bloomsbury T & T Clark, 2007.

A prayer rope on the Lord's tomb in the Holy Sepulchre